WOOD CRAFT

WOODCRAFT

MASTER THE ART OF
GREEN WOODWORKING
WITH KEY TECHNIQUES
AND INSPIRING PROJECTS

Contributors Robin Duckmanton, Tom Hepworth, Sophie Ridley, Harry Samuel, Tim Sanderson

Photographer Mark Winwood
Illustrator Andrew Torrens

Senior Editor Alastair Laing

US Editor Karyn Gerhard

Senior Designer Collette Sadler

Editorial Assistant Megan Lea

Managing Editor Dawn Henderson

Managing Art Editor Marianne Markham

Jacket Designer Steve Marsden

Senior Producer (Pre-Production) Tony Phipps

Senior Producer Luca Bazzoli

Art Director Maxine Pedliham

Publishing Director Mary-Clare Jerram

First American Edition, 2019
Published in the United States by DK Publishing
1450 Broadway, Suite 801, New York, NY 10018

Published in Great Britain by Dorling Kindersley Limited
A catalog record for this book is available from the Library of Congress.
ISBN 978-1-4654-7978-5

DK books are available at special discounts when purchased in bulk for sales promotions, premiums, fund-raising, or educational use. For details, contact: DK Publishing Special Markets, 1450 Broadway, Suite 801, New York, NY 10018; SpecialSales@dk.com

Printed and bound in China

A WORLD OF IDEAS:
SEE ALL THERE IS TO KNOW
www.dk.com

Contents

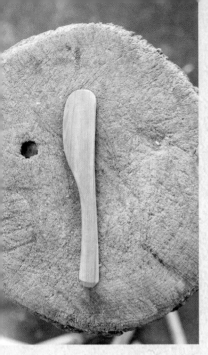

WOODCRAFT?

Woodcraft is woodwork at a human level. It relies, for the most part, upon humble folk traditions rather than machines. Using simple hand tools, perfected over millennia, keeps you close to the material and leads to a far more rewarding experience.

Crafting objects by hand develops a close relationship with the products—spending time making an everyday item such as a spoon really helps you to appreciate its form and function. By choosing to craft objects that you will use day in, day out, you are challenged to confront their functionality and their beauty.

Woodcraft also describes a more holistic approach to wood. Being in close contact with living trees, perhaps understanding them as sources of fuel or food, contributes to a wider understanding of wood culture.

In this book we have used hand tools where possible. Working in this way, you can practice your craft almost anywhere without the need to plug into electricity, and because there is less noise and dust, it can work socially. All over the world there are local spoon clubs, where groups sit around and carve together—what could be more natural than that? Crafting helps you develop a relationship with the environment,

and it can give you a different concept of existence, away from the two-dimensional world of cellphone screens. The beliefs you gain from woodcraft are both practical and philosophical: that it is better to use abrasives for sharpening tools, rather than fixing the rough surface created by blunt ones; that wood is often better cleft than sawed; and that empathy for the tools and material makes for better products.

"But why should I bother making these things when they can be bought so cheaply?" you may ask. Put simply, mass-produced items do not serve all of our needs. Whether buying the crafts of others or making objects for loved ones, the human condition finds something in craft that is not found in modern consumerism.

We have chosen projects that teach core skills and the key properties of the material. We hope that they will inform and inspire. In woodcraft, much of the joy of creating comes from interaction with the wood fibres, and seeing where the material takes back control of the shape, and how to work with that. By exploring the properties of wood, working with them to enhance the effectiveness of a product, and learning how to alter the design to make up for where the material may be lacking, you will become a well-rounded maker.

> ❝ IT IS **WIDELY** BELIEVED THAT **CRAFTING** IS **GOOD** FOR YOU. ❞

A woodworker should know the shape of the leaves on the tree from which the the wood came.

Wood

The first step in woodworking, as with any craft, is to understand your material. Green woodworking in particular calls for fresh, unseasoned wood, which is soft and pliable enough to be crafted with hand tools. The story begins with the tree.

The water content of freshly felled green wood varies between species, time of year, and other circumstances. A log can have more weight in water than from the wood itself. Once felled, and over time, this water leaves the wood until it reaches equilibrium with its environment. First to evaporate is the free water within transport fibers and cells; most shrinkage, however, occurs from the evaporation of water bound within the cellulose of cell walls. With experience, you gain a feel for when wood has dried out. When you need to be more precise, for example in joinery projects, you can weigh components to be sure: if they are kept in an airing cupboard and are no longer losing weight, they won't normally shrink any further.

These days, virtually all forestry is done with machines—often large harvesting machines as opposed to individuals with chainsaws. In the past, the management of forests and woodlands was done by hand, with more of the focus on coppicing, a traditional method of woodland management that yields smaller, more manageable products, and tends to be more popular in cultures that rely on intensively managed wood.

> 66 IN THE PAST, THE MANAGEMENT OF FORESTS AND WOODLANDS WAS DONE BY HAND. 99

A coppiced forest (also known as a copse) is an area of managed woodland that is cut on rotation, to create a useful, renewable material. Groups of young trees are cut down to near ground level—the stumps that remain are called stools. By monitoring and controlling the age a coppice stool grows to, it is possible to manage the size of the resulting product, which is often of great quality and free of knots because of fast growth from the established stool.

Life cycle of managed woodland

Managed woodlands are made up of stands—groups of trees in a specific area, usually of a similar age or size. Seedlings grow into saplings, which become poles when they grow beyond about 4in (10cm) in diameter. A single stem tree

Sustainably managed *diverse forests can provide perfect materials for woodcraft.*

within a stand or a copse is often called a standard; usually, a minimum of 20 years is required for that standard to become worthy of being turned into firewood and timber.

After 60 years of growth, a tree will usually have a diameter of about 12 in (30cm). Hardwoods and saw logs from timber trees start at about 20 in (50cm) in diameter. A 20-year-old copse grown for firewood and timber may include standards that would be grown to reach larger diameters, traditionally for lumber frames. Traditionally, each time a rotation came around, decisions would have to be made by those managing the wood about what to do with the standards—whether they should become part of the copse, or continue to be grown.

Even when it is not a coppiced forest, managed woodland tends to be planted very close together, to encourage competitive growth.

> **" THERE IS A SIGNIFICANT DIFFERENCE IN THE QUALITY OF FAST-GROWN WOOD COMPARED TO SLOW-GROWN. "**

After 20 years, it is thinned out, leaving only the stronger trees—this process is often done in several stages. In intensive forestry, trees may also be pruned to produce knot-free boards.

Growth rates

A young tree will increase its growth rate each year until it plateaus and then declines. It will continue to increase in size, but at a slower rate.

For both economical and environmental reasons, it makes sense to harvest stands when their growth rate starts to decline. Trees take the most carbon dioxide out of the atmosphere when they are growing fastest, and, when cut on rotation and managed for diversity, a useful crop can also create a fantastic habitat for wildlife.

Thinner rings do not necessarily mean less growth: the circumference of the ring has to increase with each year, so the rate of growth may be increasing though the width of the ring remains the same or even decreases.

There is a significant difference in the quality of fast-grown wood compared to slow-grown. Fast-grown wood is much stronger, particularly in terms of its tensile strength, and also denser, especially when dry. Slow-grown wood includes that found on the outer growth rings of large trees that are competing with others in the canopy. It can be lovely to carve, and often perfectly strong enough for many uses.

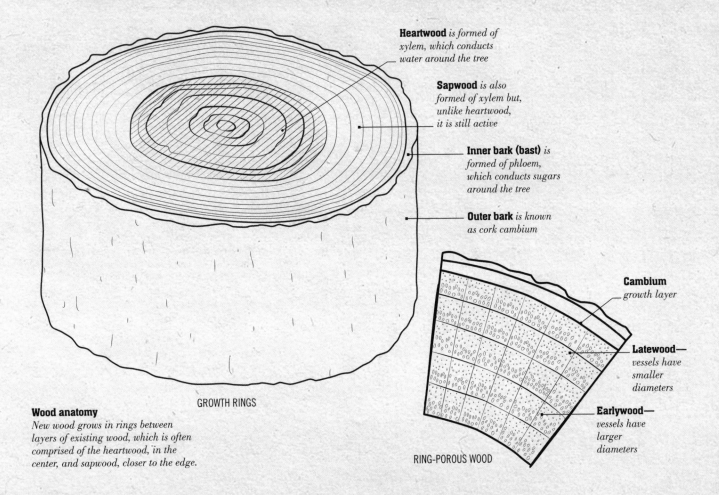

Heartwood *is formed of xylem, which conducts water around the tree*

Sapwood *is also formed of xylem but, unlike heartwood, it is still active*

Inner bark (bast) *is formed of phloem, which conducts sugars around the tree*

Outer bark *is known as cork cambium*

GROWTH RINGS

Wood anatomy
New wood grows in rings between layers of existing wood, which is often comprised of the heartwood, in the center, and sapwood, closer to the edge.

Cambium
growth layer

Latewood—
vessels have smaller diameters

Earlywood—
vessels have larger diameters

RING-POROUS WOOD

New wood

Wood is largely made up of cellulose and lignin. Cellulose provides tensile strength, and lignin offers compressional strength. Softwoods have higher lignin content than hardwoods. New wood grows between layers of existing wood (*see* Wood anatomy, above).

In species that form distinct growth rings, there are three fundamental patterns of earlywood and latewood:
- No change in cell type across the growth ring.
- A gradual reduction of the inner diameter of conducting cells from the earlywood to the latewood.
- Abrupt and distinct change in the inner diameter of conducting cells from the earlywood to the latewood.

Ring-porous wood has more vessels of larger diameter in the spring (early) growth compared to the summer (late) growth, making the rings very distinct from each other (*see* Ring-porous wood illustration, above).

In conifers, late growth is denser and remains relatively constant, whereas early growth reduces. The slow growth rate, or smaller width of growth rings, means softwoods with more rings per inch are stronger.

I would recommend softer woods for carving as greater tensile strength is often not required. However, this is not the case with furniture or the frame saw, which may need to be significantly bulkier if wood with a high tensile strength isn't used.

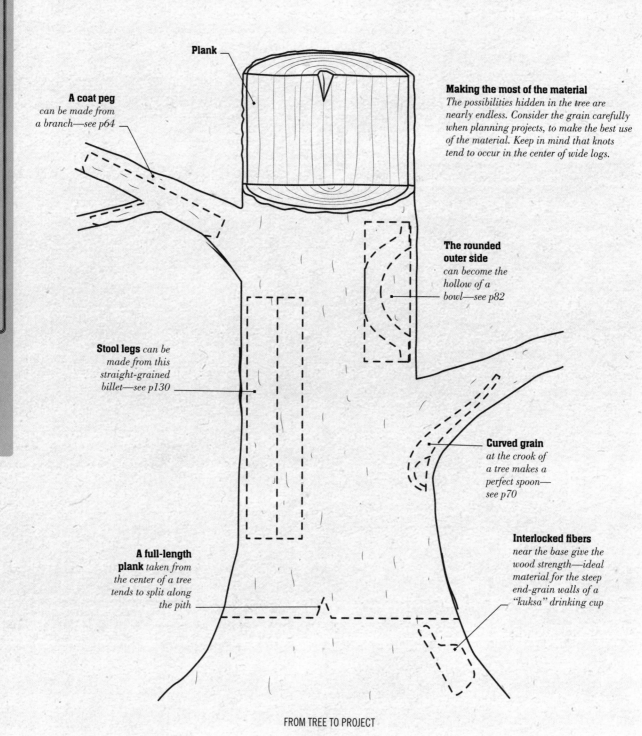

Plank

A coat peg *can be made from a branch—see p64*

Making the most of the material
The possibilities hidden in the tree are nearly endless. Consider the grain carefully when planning projects, to make the best use of the material. Keep in mind that knots tend to occur in the center of wide logs.

The rounded outer side *can become the hollow of a bowl—see p82*

Stool legs *can be made from this straight-grained billet—see p130*

Curved grain *at the crook of a tree makes a perfect spoon— see p70*

A full-length plank *taken from the center of a tree tends to split along the pith*

Interlocked fibers *near the base give the wood strength—ideal material for the steep end-grain walls of a "kuksa" drinking cup*

FROM TREE TO PROJECT

Sourcing green wood

Methods of finding or buying wood vary depending on where you live and what sort of resources are available to you, but below are a few pointers. Bear in mind that trees grown in woodlands tend to be straighter than city or park trees and have fewer knots, because they are competing against the canopy, so strive to grow upward, without many side branches.
■ Woodland is often managed by conservationists, who may remove invasive species of tree or introduce new ones to support wildlife and diversity. Contact conservationists in your area to see if they will supply wood from their management operations.
■ Firewood merchants are also a useful resource—ideally, you should get the wood before it has been sawed and split; it will often have been left in the forest for some time before being collected by a firewood merchant, but it is usually still green.
■ Find out who manages the trees in your local parks or cemeteries, and ask if any spare wood is available.
■ In non-urban areas, foresters and coppice workers are your best bet. In towns and cities, park wardens are often more useful than tree surgeons, who tend to work on difficult trees—foreign or unusual species that have been planted in gardens, or trees that are diseased. To protect buildings from possible damage caused by felling larger lengths, trees in cities are usually ringed. This means that the wood dries much more quickly, and is often wasted, though wood

> **TREES GROWN IN WOODLAND TEND TO BE STRAIGHTER THAN CITY OR PARK TREES.**

found in this way can be very useful.
■ For boards, a lumberyard is your best bet. Look for a lumber specialist who takes their time and allows you to identify the best boards –hopefully not at the bottom of the stack!

Buying blanks

You can buy cleft and sawed blanks (pieces of wood ready for carving) online from reputable suppliers, so that you know they are responsibly sourced and have the correct grain alignment and moisture content.

Storing green wood

Before buying or gathering your wood, make sure you have adequate space to store it! Small pieces of wood will remain green if kept in bags of damp shavings; avoid storing in this way for too long, as the sugars can encourage mold. Small pieces can also be kept in the freezer to keep them green. Keep larger logs green by sealing the ends with paint wax or wood glue.

CHAPTER 01

KNIFEWORK

Cut down a log or use a ready-made blank and start crafting. With a straight knife as your principal tool, work through this chapter to create practical objects and perfect key knife grips.

MAKE A
BUTTER SPREADER

This wood spreader has a wide paddle and is very light to handle: once you try it, you will never go back to metal. A spreader makes the perfect first project for learning knife skills, as the wood fibers are aligned in one flat plane, which allows you to focus on carving in the correct direction around the profile shape.

YOU WILL NEED

TOOLS & EQUIPMENT

- Pencil
- Measuring equipment
- Straight knife
- Mallet-sized log or mallet
- *optional:* Ax

MATERIALS

- 1 green wood log, about 3in (75mm) in diameter and 7in (180mm) in length

SKILLS

YOU WILL LEARN TO

- Baton (split) wood with a knife: *steps 1–2*
- Carve with a knife: *steps 3–6*
- Carve a chamfered edge: *steps 7–8, 11*

KNIFE GRIPS

- Chest lever: *p19*
- Thumb pull: *p21*
- Thumb push, pivot: *p22*

DESIGN GUIDE

When carving an object, it can be useful to follow a specific order of carving stages to hone in on the final shape. For the spreader, start by tapering the billet toward the paddle end, thinning from both sides but leaving thickness in the handle for comfort. From there, proceed to shape the profile, following the stages numbered below.

A pencil outline *is useful, but stop and assess if adjustments are needed*

2. SLOPING TOP

7in (180mm)

4. TOP CURVE

1³⁄₁₆in (30mm)

1. TAPERED PADDLE

³⁄₈in (10mm)

The bulk *of this large area of waste could be removed with an axe*

3. HANDLE

6. BACK LOWER CURVE

5. FRONT LOWER CURVE

66 THE **SPREADING** ACTION OF A **WOOD** PADDLE **CANNOT** BE BEATEN. **99**

FOCUS ON...
Running off

If you try to split off a thin billet from a thicker piece, the split will often "run off" toward the edge of the thin blank, where fibers are under greater tension. This is why it tends to be better to split sections of wood in half and then in half again until you end up with the correct size.

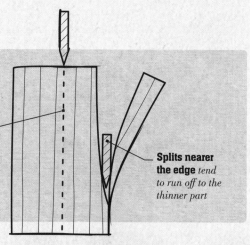

A split started *in the middle is more likely to run straight*

Splits nearer the edge *tend to run off to the thinner part*

The Process

1 Split the log

First split—or "baton"—the log in half and then half again with a knife. Make the initial split by firmly tapping on the spine of the knife with a small mallet or suitable piece of wood. Once the blade is fully embedded in the wood, continue by tapping down on the protruding point of the knife to chase the split right through the log.

Use gentle force *to tap the knife down the length of the log, which should split along the grain*

2 Baton out a blank

You are aiming to take a full width plank from the side of a quartered log. To reduce the risk of running off (*see* above), first split the quarter in two, making sure what's left is large enough that when split in two again you have a little plank around ⅜in (10mm); this will be your carving piece, or "blank." Wood split along the radius of the log in this way—called "radial"—is less likely to cup (*see* p103) as it dries because the grain is relatively straight.

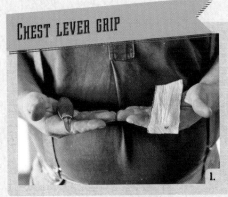

CHEST LEVER GRIP

1. Place the handle of the knife in the palm of your gripping hand, blade edge facing out, then close your fingers and raise your hands up to rest on your chest. Your fingernails should face upward and your knuckles act as a pivot on your chest.

2. To make cuts, lock your wrists and pull your shoulders back while pushing your ribcage up and out. Aim to move both knife and blank in a mirrored action, like a pair of scissors, your arms acting as levers turning on the fulcrum of your chest.

3 Start on the paddle

As per the order of carving on p16, the first stage is to create the paddle taper by thinning down wood at one end, using the knife in chest lever grip; *see* above. Start to take shavings on the left-hand side of the blank, from just under halfway along its length. Make an angled cut that takes off the corner of the blank edge, to create a "facet." Then cut another facet that takes off the corners of the first. The process of whittling is, in essence, cutting a series of facets that take off corners and high points.

4 Taper the paddle

Continue cutting facets across the width of the blank, then turn it over and cut the same facets on the other side. Regularly turn the blank over as you whittle, to take off even amounts of wood on both sides. Take more wood off as you progress toward the end of the blank, so that you create a tapering profile to a thin end of about ⅟₁₆in (2mm).

Engage the blade *near the tip to make cuts to the far side of the blank*

CONTINUED ☞

TIP

For speed, you could remove the substantial amount of waste wood under the handle with an axe; *see* Shaping with an axe, p50.

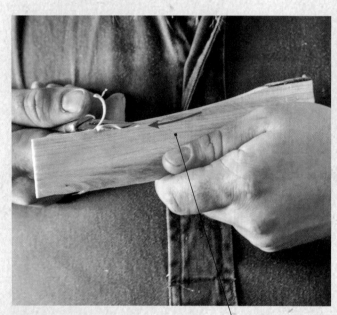

5 Shape the sloping top

Still using chest lever grip, make cuts along one of the long edges of the blank to form the profile of the top of the spreader. You are aiming to shape a shallow concave that descends from the handle end and rises slightly as it approaches the paddle end.

Make shallow *cuts for fine shaping*

6 Shape the handle

Holding the blank at the paddle end, form a handle about ⁹⁄₁₆in (15mm) wide by removing waste from the base side. Still in chest lever grip, start cuts from just under halfway along the blank, from what will be the start of the paddle. Cut a concave that starts fairly steeply and then levels out for the handle shaft, before rising again slightly at the handle end.

You will see *the basic shape of the spreader start to take form*

THUMB PULL GRIP

1. Hold the knife in your fingertips, with your forefinger high up on the handle and your palm open and empty.

2. Close your fingers onto your palm. Keep your thumb out of the direction of the cut by positioning it at 10 o'clock to the blade's 12 o'clock; or at 2 o'clock if you are left-handed.

1.

2.

Position your thumb *so that it is offset from the blade as you squeeze the grip*

7 Facet the handle and paddle

Before moving on to the paddle, create a more rounded shape to the handle by cutting a series of eight facets down its length, shaving off all of the corners to form a squashed octagon shape when seen in cross section. Turn the blank around and continue the same series of facets to round off the corners of the paddle.

Aim to cut *single long shavings for a smooth finish*

8 Chamfer the handle

Now neaten the end of the handle by cutting a 45° bevel all the way around—known as a "chamfer"— using the thumb pull grip; *see* above. Chamfering not only gives a neat appearance, but by taking off square edges it also makes surfaces more comfortable to grip.

CONTINUED ☞

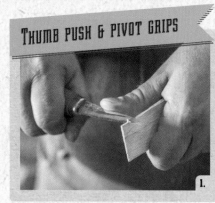

THUMB PUSH & PIVOT GRIPS

1. For thumb push, place your clenched thumb level with where you want to start the cut. Put your thumb on the back of the knife, in the middle offset from the tip, which makes the cut engage the blade. Push it forward by extending your thumb.

2. For thumb pivot, instead of pushing with your thumb, keep it still so that it acts as a pivot for the cutting movement made by the wrist of your other hand.

9 Curve the paddle
Use thumb push grip to cut the curved shape of the paddle; *see above*. Curve the top of the paddle first, then the lower curve at the front, followed by the lower curve at the back as it blends into the handle. Don't attempt to cut curves in one or two deep shavings. Knock off a corner first, then shave off the corners of this first cut, and so on; as the curve starts to form, you can take off longer shavings.

Shape a long curve *at the base and a shorter, shallower curve at the top*

10 Dress the surface
Create a smooth finish—or "dress"—to the flat faces of the paddle. Employ thumb push grip for an initial cleanup, then switch to thumb pivot grip for finer cuts; *see above*.

Remove any *rough patches, high points, and nicks*

TIP

Removing sharp edges by cutting chamfers prevents the wood fibers from rising and becoming "furry" with use.

Design variations

While staying in the same flat plane, play around with shape and scale to create other useful kitchen utensils. Build in functionality by thinking hard about what jobs the utensil will be called on to do.

SPATULA

Optional hole *can be drilled and chamfered, for hanging on a hook*

Wide chamfer *cut into the paddle edge for flipping food*

JAM SPREADER

Pointed end *to the paddle for scraping in the corners of jars*

Steep "crank," *or midsection, to help with the scooping action*

11 Round off edges

Finally, return to thumb push grip and cut a chamfer along the edges of the butter spreader paddle (the handle has already been chamfered), to remove sharp edges and create a comfortable, neat finish.

Take long, *thin shavings for a neat chamfered edge*

MAKE A
TOGGLE

Carving a toggle is a fantastic way to improvise a simple and effective fastener. They can be used in a variety of ways—for example, in conjunction with short loops of material to use as a button on a duffle coat, or for drawing through and knotting off a length of cord to open and close a bag.

YOU WILL NEED

TOOLS AND EQUIPMENT

- Bench hook
- Handsaw (such as a pull saw)
- Straight knife
- Small mallet
- Electric drill

MATERIALS

- A branch, about 1³⁄₁₆in (30mm) in diameter and at least 2½in (64mm) long, but longer is convenient to hold and allows for multiple toggles
- Cord

SKILLS

YOU WILL LEARN TO

- Cut with a pull saw: *step 6*
- Use an electric drill: *step 2*

REMIND YOURSELF HOW TO

- Baton (split) wood with a knife: *p16*
- Carve with a knife: *p16*
- Carve a chamfered edge: *p16*

KNIFE GRIPS

- Chest lever: *p19*
- Thumb pivot: *p22*

DESIGN GUIDE

The lozengelike horizontal design creates a sturdy toggle, strong without being too cumbersome. The tapered ends enable it to be used like a handle and easily slip through a loop or buttonhole; they also make the toggle comfortable to hold and introduce a pleasing curvature to the aesthetic.

Notch provides *recess where cord sits flush when loose*

Ends given a *chamfered point*

2⅜in (60mm)

1. FACETED MAIN BODY

¾in (19mm)

4. CHAMFERED ENDS

Sides taper mainly *along their width, only slightly in their depth*

OVERHEAD VIEW

3. TAPERED SIDES

2. RECESSED NOTCH

Holes drilled *to match the size of intended cord*

66 IMPROVING THE **FUNCTIONALITY** OF THREAD, CORDAGE, AND ROPE WITH THE **ADDITION** OF **WHITTLED** WOODEN ARTIFACTS IS AN **ANCIENT TECHNOLOGY**, AND NO LESS USEFUL TODAY. 99

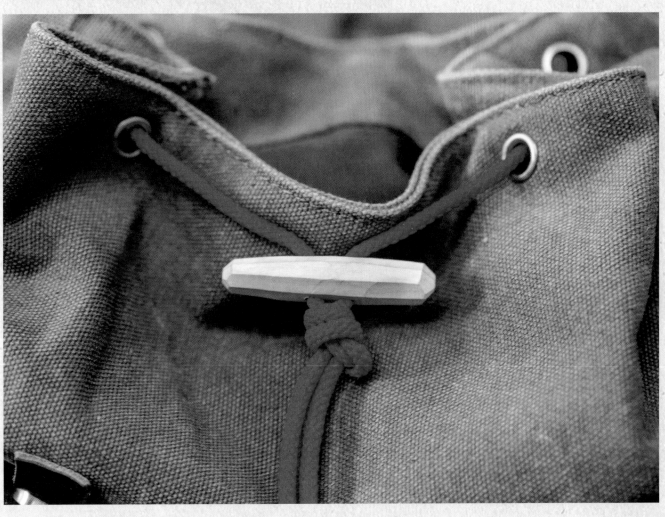

USING A PULL SAW

Saw blades can jump when starting a cut, but the risk is greatly reduced once at least three teeth are in contact. To avoid a jump, start by drawing the blade in the opposite direction to the sawing action—with a pull saw, by pushing it—to gently create a slot for the teeth to rest in.

Rest your thumb on the top edge of the blade to steady and control initial cuts.

A bench hook provides space for cutting and an edge to work to, and enables you to hold the object steady.

The Process

1 Size the wood
Cut a section of wood from the branch with a pull saw (*see* above), leaving enough excess so that it is easy to grip when carving. Baton the section in half vertically with a knife.

Technique: Batoning with a knife—see p16

Aim to split *down the middle, through the pith*

2 Drill holes
Drill a pair of holes through one of the halves. The diameter of the drill bit depends on the thickness of cord: neither too loose nor so tight that it is difficult to thread. Make sure the holes are centered, about ¾in (19mm) from the edge, and try to drill straight down (but *see* Truing angled holes, above right). Minimize "tear out" by drilling through into some scrap wood.

Drilling holes exactly straight can be difficult. If your holes have ended up slanted, remedy the situation by truing to the angle of the holes. To do this, make cuts to the top and bottom of the toggle at such an angle that the faces end up perpendicular to the drilled holes.

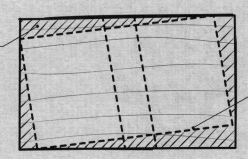

Shave down *at an angle corresponding to the slant of the hole*

New faces *at the top and bottom are now 90° to the hole*

Shave down *until the pith is no longer showing*

3 Smooth off

Turning to your knife, employ the chest lever grip to smooth off any tear out caused by drilling the holes. At the same time, remove the pith and some of the youngest growth wood with the tightest rings, which, if left in, make the toggle more prone to splitting.

Knife grip: Chest lever—see p19

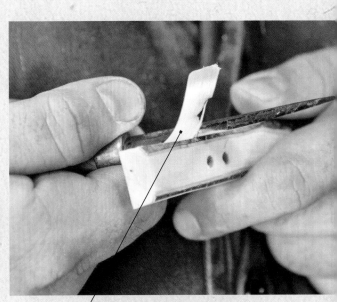

Try to cut *single, long shavings for a smooth finish*

4 Facet the toggle

Still with chest lever, remove the bark and start shaping the toggle by cutting a series of facets down its length: two wide facets top and bottom, then six thinner facets connecting them, to create the curved sides—you are aiming for a squashed octagon shape in cross section. If need be, "true" the toggle so that the holes are perfectly straight; *see* Truing angled holes, above.

CONTINUED ☞

PENCIL GRIP

Hold the sides of the knife as you would a pencil, resting the handle in the crook of your hand.

Make gentle cuts by moving the blade with finger and thumb, just as with writing. Keep everything steady: rest your hand on the bench and hold the toggle firmly.

Take care! Your fingers will be close to the sharp edge of the blade. Keep all fingers out of the direction of cut in case the knife slips.

Pull the cord
tight to test the notch depth

5 Cut a notch
Holding the knife with pencil grip (*see* above), cut a shallow notch between the holes on one side of the toggle. Carve out the notch with the tip of the knife, resting the toggle on a work surface. The notch should be deep enough to allow the cord to sit flush when threaded.

6 Saw to size
Place the toggle on the bench hook and saw off the excess wood, ensuring the holes are centered in the toggle. The excess can be used to make more toggles.

> **THE JOY** OF MAKING FUNCTIONAL OBJECTS LIES IN THE **USING**. AS YOU **ENGAGE** WITH THE **DESIGN** YOU CAN **PERFECT** IT OVER TIME. **"**

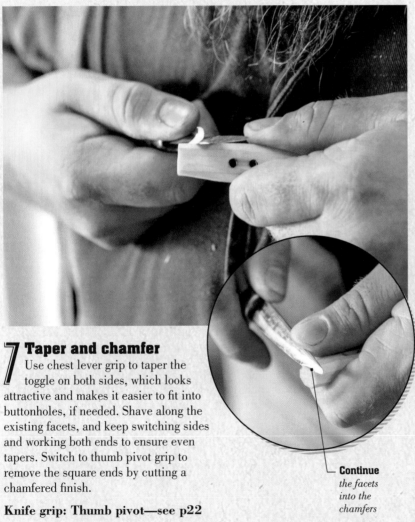

7 Taper and chamfer
Use chest lever grip to taper the toggle on both sides, which looks attractive and makes it easier to fit into buttonholes, if needed. Shave along the existing facets, and keep switching sides and working both ends to ensure even tapers. Switch to thumb pivot grip to remove the square ends by cutting a chamfered finish.

Knife grip: Thumb pivot—see p22

Technique: Carving a chamfered edge—see p16

Continue *the facets into the chamfers*

Design variations
The simplicity of toggles makes them endlessly adaptable. Folk craft often looks for ways to incorporate sculpture into functional pieces, such as with this fish-shaped light pull design.

BARREL TOGGLE

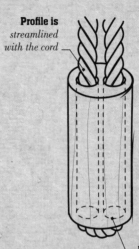

Profile is *streamlined with the cord*

Barrel shape *locates strength in the toggle's thickness*

FISH LIGHT PULL

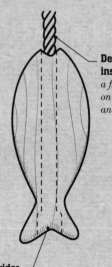

Design inspired *by a fish caught on a hook and line*

Hole is wider *at the base for fitting a knot*

BANGLE

A wooden bangle is light and comfortable on the wrist. Wood grain can present some remarkable natural patterns, especially a section of highly figured spalted wood with dark lines left by fungal infection. Removing the central rings is an effective way to prevent the wood from splitting as it dries.

YOU WILL NEED

TOOLS & EQUIPMENT
- Plywood
- Auger (or electric drill and frame saw)
- Straight knife
- Measuring equipment
- Pencil
- Mallet or mallet-sized log

MATERIALS
- Disk of green wood, about 3^{15}⁄₁₆in (100mm) in diameter and 1^{3}⁄₁₆in (30mm) thick (but be led by the wearer)

SKILLS

YOU WILL LEARN TO
- Use an auger: *step 1*
- Make circular cuts with a knife and produce rounded shaping: *steps 2, 5–7*
- Account for wood shrinkage: *step 3*

REMIND YOURSELF HOW TO
- Baton with a knife: *p16*

KNIFE GRIPS
- Reinforced pull: *p32*
- Chest lever: *p19*
- Thumb pull: *p21*

DESIGN GUIDE

The exact size of hole will be determined by the practicalities of fit, but personal choice can be exercised in the thickness and, to some degree, the shaping, depending on the style aimed for: chunky and bold, or sleek and elegant?

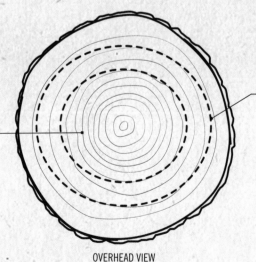

Center the bangle *around the annular rings to ensure even shrinkage*

An oval shape *allows for the smallest bangle, since a hand can compress to an oval profile*

OVERHEAD VIEW

“ BANGLES MUST BE **CARVED** WITH THE **WEARER** ALWAYS IN MIND. ”

REINFORCED PULL GRIP

Grip the knife with the blade's tip vertical and your thumb resting on the blunt back. Be sure to stay clear of the protruding tip.

Reinforce the grip by clasping your cutting hand with your supporting hand.

Rotate the blade edge anticlockwise around the interior surface, or rotate clockwise if you are left handed.

The Process

Steady the disk *against your chest*

2 Expand the hole
Use a knife to expand and shape the hole, employing the reinforced pull grip; *see* above. Don't try to take single cuts of the full circumference: stop when your wrist hits your chest and rotate the disk to take the next cut. If shaping an oval, take more material from two of the opposite quadrants.

The screw pushes *wood shavings out of the hole as the auger turns*

1 Cut the starter hole
Rest the disk on a spare piece of ply or other wood, to protect both the auger blade and the floor. Holding the disk steady with your feet, position the auger in the center of the annular rings and turn the T-handle clockwise, all the time keeping it straight, until you've cut through.

TIP
If you don't have an auger, use an electric drill instead. You can also use a frame or coping saw to expand the hole.

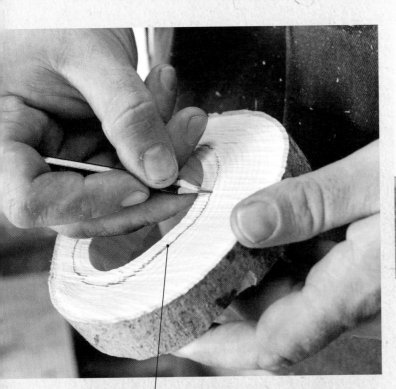

Try drawing freehand *or join up a series of dots at the correct width*

3 Draw a guideline

Once happy with the size of the hole, mark a pencil line for the width, parallel to the edge of the hole. Take into account the shrinkage as the wood dries out: 10 percent is a good rule of thumb; for example, if you are aiming for 3⁹⁄₁₆in (90mm) diameter, you should draw a line at 3¹⁵⁄₁₆in (100mm).

4 Baton to size

If the disk is significantly wider than the intended bangle, you can speed up the shaping process by batoning the wood roughly to size. Work around the disk, splitting off sections, but be sure to leave enough waste around the guideline for fine shaping. At this point, leave the piece to dry for two weeks.

Technique: Batoning with a knife—see p16

Tap the point *of the knife with the mallet*

CONTINUED ☞

FOCUS ON...
RATES OF DRYING

Wood fibers at varied rates along the different axes. Removing central rings allows the wood to "move," hence avoiding splits that happen when the wood tries to change shape but can't without pulling itself apart.

Radial splits *occur because faster shrinkage on the tangent starts to pull the wood apart*

TANGENT 8%

RADIUS 4%

Radial shrinkage *is half that of tangential*

LONGITUDE 0.3%

RADIAL SPLITS

RATES OF SHRINKAGE

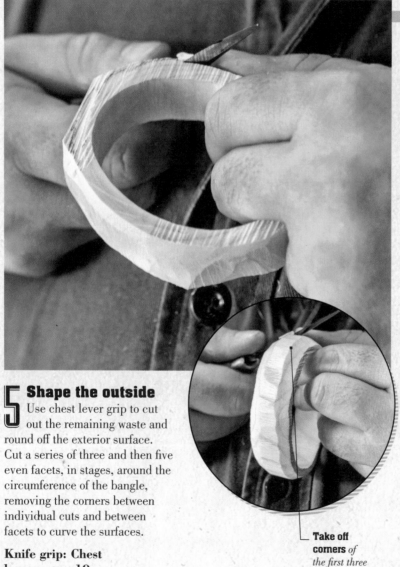

5 Shape the outside
Use chest lever grip to cut out the remaining waste and round off the exterior surface. Cut a series of three and then five even facets, in stages, around the circumference of the bangle, removing the corners between individual cuts and between facets to curve the surfaces.

Knife grip: Chest lever—see p19

Take off corners *of the first three facets to curve the surface*

6 Neaten the sides
Switch to the thumb pull grip to smooth off the rough-sawn surface around the edge of the bangle, tidying up both sides. Keep your thumbs safely tucked away behind the bangle.

Knife grip: Thumb pull—see p21

> *" CARVING THE ROUNDED SHAPE IS MADE EASIER BECAUSE YOU ARE NOT WORKING ACROSS THE END GRAIN. "*

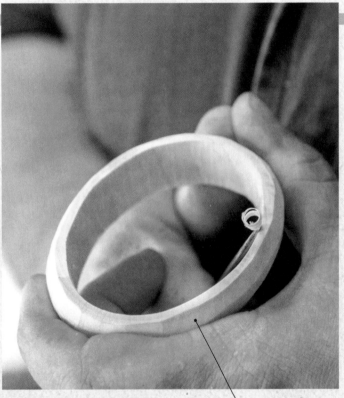

Gently rotate
*the bangle as
you make cuts*

7 Shape the inside
Finally, return to the reinforced pull stroke to carve a convex surface on the inside of the bangle, rounding off the corners to mirror the five-faceted shape to the exterior of the bangle.

Design variations
Once you have perfected carving a basic ring, you can get creative by adapting the size and exterior shape, and by introducing a taper, to produce different useful artefacts.

NAPKIN RING

A narrow hole *is better for clasping the napkin*

Experiment *with a more angular shape for the exterior*

EGG CUP

Hole size *will depend on the kind of eggs you like—hen, duck, or goose!*

Mimic the shape *of an egg by tapering to a wider top edge*

MAKE A
COFFEE BAG CLIP

This project makes use of the tensile strength and elastic properties of wood. Understanding these properties, and manipulating them to create an effective clip, will teach you many valuable lessons that can be used in other projects.

YOU WILL NEED

TOOLS & EQUIPMENT
- Electric drill and ⁹⁄₁₆in (15mm) drill bit
- Clamp
- Crosscut saw
- Straight knife

MATERIALS
- A green wood rod, about 1½in (38mm) in diameter and at least 5⅞in (150mm) long, but a longer rod makes it much easier to saw in step 1

SKILLS

YOU WILL LEARN TO
- Make a "rip" cut: *step 1*
- Shape wood in order to make it flexible: *steps 3–7*

REMIND YOURSELF HOW TO
- Use an electric drill: *p24*
- Carve with a knife: *p16*
- Carve a chamfered edge: *p16*

KNIFE GRIPS
- Thumb pull: *p21*
- Reinforced pull: *p32*
- Forehand: *p39*
- Chest lever: *p19*
- Thumb pivot: *p22*

DESIGN GUIDE

The key practical issue with wooden clips is that, with use, the split required to form the clasp has a natural tendency to continue up through the head of the clip. This design finds a simple and elegant solution to the problem by drilling a hole to spread the force of the split.

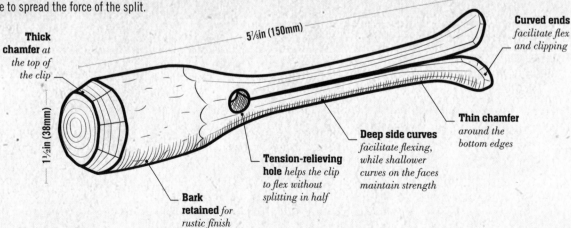

Thick chamfer *at the top of the clip*

1½in (38mm)

5⅞in (150mm)

Curved ends *facilitate flex and clipping*

Thin chamfer *around the bottom edges*

Deep side curves *facilitate flexing, while shallower curves on the faces maintain strength*

Tension-relieving hole *helps the clip to flex without splitting in half*

Bark retained *for rustic finish*

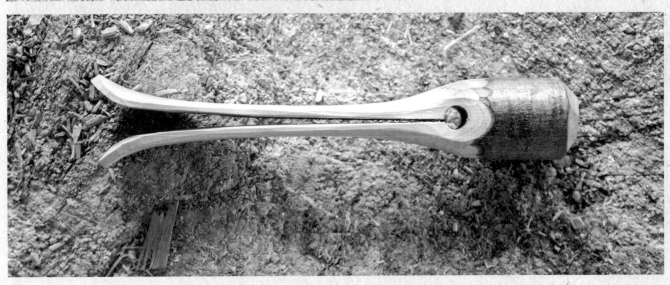

❝ TIME WAS WHEN EVERY **HOUSEHOLD** WAS HOME TO **WHITTLED OBJECTS.❞**

FOCUS ON...
RELIEVING PRESSURE

If you were just to saw down the center of the rod without having first drilled a hole, the clip would almost certainly split right down into two pieces during use. The hole spreads out the area where the splitting pressure is directed, meaning the top of the clip is much stronger, and won't need reinforcing.

Pressure from
the split is spread out by the hole

HOLE CLIP

All force
directed to a single point, causing split

NON-HOLE CLIP

The Process

1 Drill and saw the rod
Drill a hole through the center of the rod 4¹⁵⁄₁₆in (125mm) from an end. Clamp the rod to a work surface and saw vertically through the middle down to the hole. Sawing along the wood fibers like this is called "ripping." Saw the rod off about 1in (25mm) beyond the hole.

Technique: Using an electric drill—see p24

— **To help sight**
the saw line, leave the drill bit in the hole as a guide

2 Chamfer the top and peel off the bark
Switching to knifework, employ thumb pull grip to cut a neat chamfer at the top of the clip. Then remove most of the bark using mainly the reinforced grip, pivoting your wrist to make cuts. Leave a strip of bark between the chamfer and the hole. Switch to forehand grip to remove bark at the ends; *see* above right.

Technique: Carving a chamfered edge—see p16

Knife grips: Thumb pull, Reinforced pull—see pp21, 32

— **Cut a thick chamfer**
and shave off the sawn surface, too

Hold the wood in your non-dominant hand, across your thigh. Make a fist around the handle of the knife and point the blade diagonally upward.

To make shavings, move the knife away from your body along the surface of the wood.

TIP
Cutting curves into the sides and faces enables the clip to flex along its length.

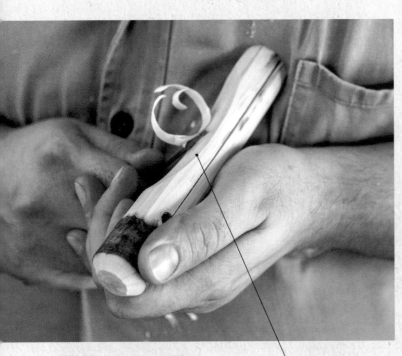

Take off thin *shavings, and ensure the clip ends up symmetrical*

3 Shape the sides
Employ the reinforced grip to shape the outer parts of the clip, taking out the midsection of each side in a smooth curve, and leaving both ends at their full width. Carve from the end of the curve to the center, then turn the clip around and carve in the same direction from the opposite end.

4 Shape the front and back
In the same way, shave down the front and back faces of the clip, but do not shave off too much: create a more shallow concave than on the sides. Again, leave the ends at full thickness.

Center the concave *at the midpoint of the clip, as with the sides*

CONTINUED ☞

TIP
If the wood is very wet, dab wood glue on the top cut surface to slow drying and reduce the risk of splits; carve off once the wood has fully dried.

> **AS YOU CARVE YOUR CLIP, FOCUS ON CREATING SMOOTH LINES AND A SYMMETRICAL APPEARANCE.**

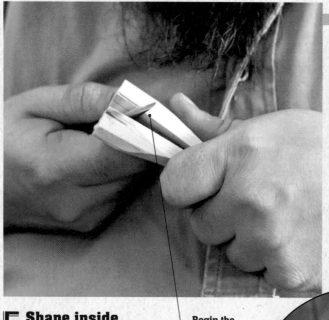

Begin the curve *about ¾in (19mm) from the end*

5 Shape inside the ends

Employ chest lever grip to remove material from inside the ends of the clip. Gradually work your way in and shape matching convex curves on both sides. Switch to thumb pivot grip to finesse the line of each curve.

Knife grips: Chest lever, thumb pivot—see pp19, 22

Blend the shape *of the ends into the curved sides and front and back faces*

6 Chamfer and shape the outsides

Remove the sharp edges at the ends by cutting a thin chamfer. Use a combination of thumb pivot grip for the sides and thumb pull for the very ends, to create a smooth edge. Switch to reinforced grip to remove material from outside of the ends, this time shaping concave lines parallel to the inside convex curves.

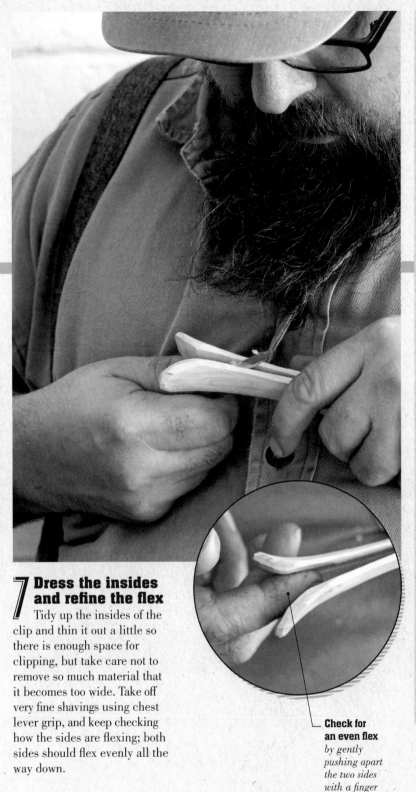

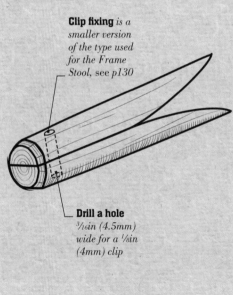

Design variations

Rather than trying to prevent the clip from splitting, these alternative designs accept the likelihood of splitting and incorporate solutions to hold the two sides together.

GYPSY CLIP

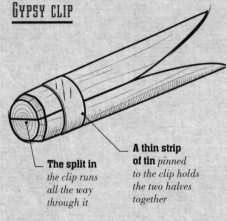

The split in *the clip runs all the way through it*

A thin strip of tin *pinned to the clip holds the two halves together*

PEGGED CLIP

Clip fixing *is a smaller version of the type used for the Frame Stool, see p130*

Drill a hole *³⁄₁₆in (4.5mm) wide for a ¹⁄₈in (4mm) clip*

7 Dress the insides and refine the flex
Tidy up the insides of the clip and thin it out a little so there is enough space for clipping, but take care not to remove so much material that it becomes too wide. Take off very fine shavings using chest lever grip, and keep checking how the sides are flexing; both sides should flex evenly all the way down.

Check for an even flex *by gently pushing apart the two sides with a finger*

MAKE A
PULLED FIBER BRUSH

At its essence wood is a fibrous material, and this project offers a great way to explore and make use of this quality. As you form both the bristles of the brush and the woven binding holding them together, you are stretching the properties of the wood almost to breaking point, yet creating an object that is simple, functional, and beautiful.

YOU WILL NEED

TOOLS & EQUIPMENT
- Straight knife
- Small mallet
- *optional*: Handsaw (such as a pull saw)

MATERIALS
- 2 green wood rods, about $^{13}/_{16}$in (30mm) in diameter; $11^{13}/_{16}$in (300mm) long for the brush and $39^{3}/_{8}$in (1000mm) long for the binding

SKILLS

YOU WILL LEARN TO
- Pull unbroken lengths of wood fibers: *steps 1–4*
- Split a rod down to a pliable strip: *steps 5–6*
- Weave with a wood strip: *step 7*

REMIND YOURSELF HOW TO
- Use a pull saw: *p24*
- Carve a chamfered edge: *p16*
- Baton with a knife: *p16*

KNIFE GRIPS
- Forehand: *p39*
- Thumb pull: *p21*

DESIGN GUIDE

The bristles of the brush are formed by pulling apart the wood into its constituent fibers. The central band of rod, left intact, acts as anchor to the fibers, enabling the rod to be stripped from both ends to create a thick head of bristles leaving behind an ergonomic handle.

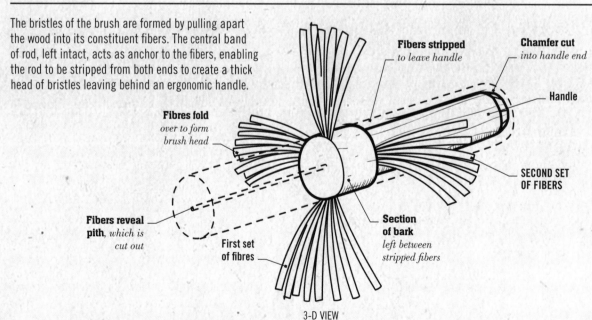

Fibers stripped *to leave handle*

Chamfer cut *into handle end*

Handle

Fibres fold *over to form brush head*

SECOND SET OF FIBERS

Fibers reveal pith, *which is cut out*

First set of fibres

Section of bark *left between stripped fibers*

3-D VIEW

FOCUS ON...
STRIPPING WOOD FIBERS

Wood fibers have a natural tendency to "run off"; *see* p18. Here, once you have worked around the stick pulling off short fibers, there are then enough layers so that even though the peeled fibers run off, the bonds between layers are strong enough to maintain them as a strip.

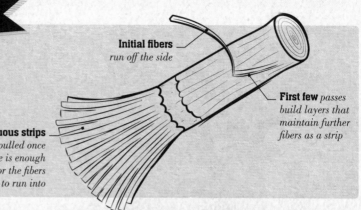

Initial fibers *run off the side*

First few *passes build layers that maintain further fibers as a strip*

Continuous strips *can be pulled once there is enough wood for the fibers to run into*

The Process

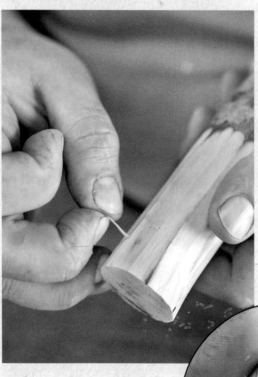

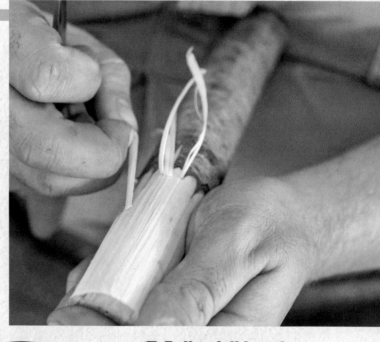

1 Start off the fibers
Using forehand grip, shave bark from a third of the rod, being careful to remove as little wood as possible. Pluck at fibers at the sawn end with the blade tip, and start pulling off slithers.

Knife grips: Forehand, thumb pull—see pp39, 21

Use thumb pull grip *to pluck fibers*

2 Pull to full length
The first slithers will quickly run off to the sides and tear out. Keep plucking with the knife and pulling with your fingers, moving around the circumference of the rod, until eventually you are able to pull fibers down the entire length. This may take several passes and must not be rushed, since we are relying on the natural running off of fibers to set the conditions for finally being able to draw the fibers in long strips.

Cut diagonally *through the pith, then pare it back*

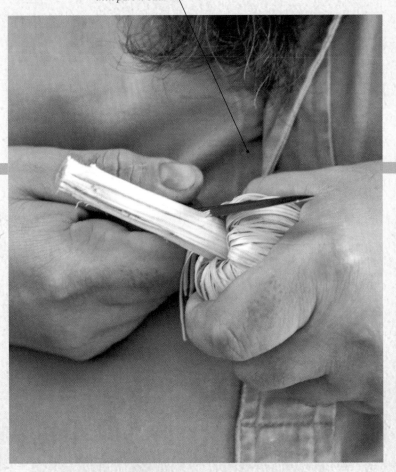

Fold back over *the first set of fibers*

Thicker fibers *can be split in half again*

◪ Cut off the pith

Continue going around and around the rod, plucking and pulling the fibers. Eventually there will be no more full-length fibers to pull, and you will hit the pith at the center. At this point, simply cut off the pith with the knife in chest lever grip, or saw it off with a pull saw.

Knife grip: Chest lever—see p19

Technique: Using a pull saw—see p24

◪ Strip the handle side

Shave bark off the other half, stopping ¾in (19mm) from the first fibers to leave a band of bark. Repeat steps 1–3, but stop pulling fibers when the rod reaches a diameter of about ¾in (19mm) to leave a handle. Cut a chamfer at the end of the handle using thumb pull grip.

Technique: Cutting a chamfered finish—see p16

CONTINUED ☞

WEAVING THE BINDING

1. Take one end of the strip, form a loop big enough to squeeze on to the bristles but small enough to hold position, then tightly tie in the end.

2. Take the other end of the strip and weave it through and around the original loop, making several passes, if necessary, until you are happy with the thickness and strength of the loop.

Adjust the tension *on either side to run the split straight*

Fiber tension *stops the split running off to the side*

5 Baton the second rod

The binding ring is created from the same material as the brush, split over and over again until you have a thin ribbon. First baton the rod in half, starting the split with a knife and small mallet, and continuing with your hands. You need to control the split by putting tension into the side you wish the split to run into. A great way to do this is by bracing each side of the split with your thumbs.

Technique: Batoning with a knife—see p16

6 Split down to a pliable strip

Keep splitting the wood in half and half again. When splitting a thinner splint from a larger one, you can focus all of your efforts into stretching the thick side by using both arms to bend the stick across your knee. Keep splitting until you end up with a thin, fairly pliable strip of wood.

7 Weave a binding ring

Work a shallow bend into the strip by bending it around your knee, then make tighter bends with your fingers, working along the strip, until it is flexible enough to be woven. Weave the strip into a ring that fits tightly over the top of the fibers; *see* Weaving the binding, above left. Gently pull the ends to tighten the ring, then cut off the excess.

Cut off *the ends using thumb pull grip*

Design variations

Once you've got the knack of stripping fibers you can experiment with different brush sizes. Or try a more rough-and-ready way of delaminating wood to make a renewable alternative to a scouring pad.

LONG-HANDLED BROOM

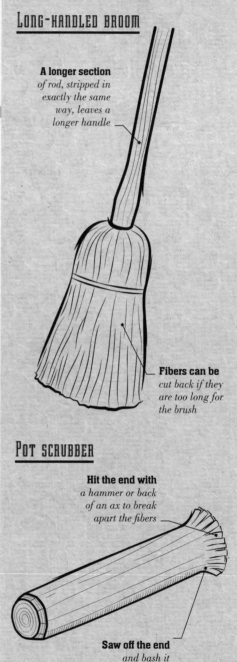

A longer section *of rod, stripped in exactly the same way, leaves a longer handle*

Fibers can be *cut back if they are too long for the brush*

POT SCRUBBER

Hit the end with *a hammer or back of an ax to break apart the fibers*

Saw off the end *and bash it again to renew the scrubber*

CHAPTER 02
AXWORK

All the projects in this chapter have as their starting point splitting a log and shaping with an ax. As you work through, you will develop increasing precision and tackle simple joinery.

MAKE A
MALLET

A large mallet is an essential tool for hitting an ax, a froe, or wedges to split logs. Mallets take a fair beating in their lifetime, and will often wear through until the end is too weak; if this happens, simply saw off the end to leave a smaller mallet. Wooden mallets must be used on axes and metal wedges, rather than metal hammers, which are more likely to deform the wedge and can produce dangerous flying metal splinters.

YOU WILL NEED

TOOLS & EQUIPMENT
- Handsaw
- Ax block
- Ax
- Straight knife

MATERIALS
- 1 log of green wood, approximately $4\frac{5}{16}$in (110mm) in diameter and 20in (500mm) in length; a softer wood will be easier to carve, but a harder wood will make a more enduring mallet

SKILLS

YOU WILL LEARN TO
- Saw a log with a handsaw: *step 2*
- Shape with an ax: *steps 3–5*

REMIND YOURSELF HOW TO
- Carve a chamfered edge: *p16*

KNIFE GRIPS
- Thumb pull: *p21*
- Forehand: *p39*

DESIGN GUIDE

Try to select a log with a knotty section for the hitting end of the mallet. Size the handle according to what's comfortable for you to grip, though any less than 1½in (38mm) will make it too weak.

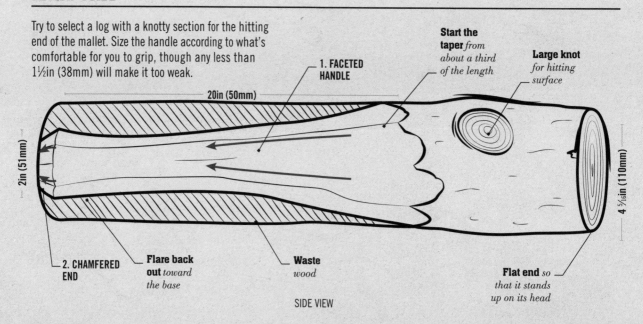

1. FACETED HANDLE

Start the taper *from about a third of the length*

Large knot *for hitting surface*

20in (50mm)

2in (51mm)

$4\frac{5}{16}$in (110mm)

2. CHAMFERED END

Flare back out *toward the base*

Waste *wood*

Flat end *so that it stands up on its head*

SIDE VIEW

FOCUS ON...

KNOTTY WOOD

Knots are grain configurations where there was once a branch growing out. They can be from a live branch or from a dead one absorbed into the trunk, called a "dead knot." Wood is weaker and most likely to split or delaminate on straight sections. Knotty grain is at an angle and interlocked with the straight grain, which prevents splitting from occuring so quickly.

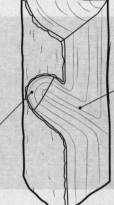

Interlocked grain
is harder and less likely to split when used as a hitting surface

Side branch
forms a knot in the log

The Process

The twisted grain *of knotty wood makes it more resilient*

1 Choose the billet
Assess the log and identify the section of wood you want for the mallet. Ideally, it should be a knotty section to provide a harder impact area for the hitting face, but with knot-free wood above or below for the handle; *see* Knotty wood, above.

2 Saw the billet
Use a handsaw to cut out the billet. Place the log on an ax block, resting the knee of your supporting side on the log to steady it and using your thumb or index finger to guide the blade. Saw as close to the edge of the block as possible to prevent the wood from tipping, and saw downward at about a 45° angle; if you tried to saw horizontally, the log would simply roll on the block.

l. Chopping cuts create chips by cutting across the fibers at an angle of around 30°, which the wedge of the ax then splits along the grain.

2. A more vertical action with gentler force can then be used to remove the chips and make finer cuts. These shaving cuts use the bevel of the blade to guide the cutting edge, allowing greater control.

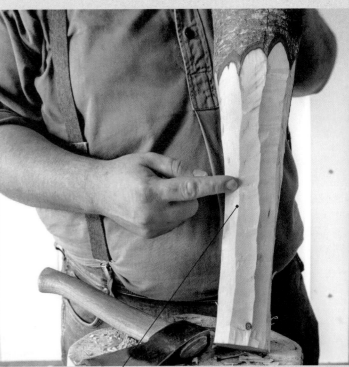

Make the **facets** *fairly neat and uniform*

3 Rough shape the handle

Begin to square and shape the handle, starting cuts from just below the knotty head. When taking thick shavings, it may help to lever open the previous cut before taking the next swing, giving you a wider target; or leave the ax in the cut and bump both ax and mallet down on the block, to split wood off.

Start to taper *the handle toward the mallet base*

4 Facet the handle

Take off the corners of your initial shaping and refine the handle by cutting a series of eight facets, so that it has a roughly octagonal shape viewed in cross section. Make the facets broadly equal in width, with the edges running in parallel lines toward the end; if the handle tapers too much it can be hard to hold.

CONTINUED ☞

054
055

Keep your thumb
*offset from the
direction of the
blade and tucked
behind the handle*

5 Shave down to size

Once you've shaped your eight sides, keep shaving them down in turn to reduce the width of the handle until it's comfortable to grip but not so thin that it loses strength. As you reduce the girth, also shape the handle so that it flares out slightly toward the bottom, rather than tapering to a point.

Try to give
*the surfaces as
smooth a finish
as possible*

6 Chamfer the end

Cut a chamfer at the handle's end; this prevents the wood from chipping and improves the comfort of the grip. The top of the mallet could also be chamfered, but make the chamfer much thinner so that the mallet can still be stored balanced on its head.

Technique: Carving a chamfered edge—see p16

Knife grip: Thumb pull—see p21

Cut off the *corners to give a 45° bevel*

7 Dress the handle

Finally, take off any untidy edges, sharp points, and rough patches from the handle. The forehand grip works well for this, as it allows you to take off long, thin shavings. Resting the mallet on an ax block, position the knife at a slight diagonal with the tip pointing upward, and simply shave down the length of the handle, cutting with the part of the blade closest to the handle.

Knife grip: Forehand—see p39

Design variations

The split-log mallet is easier to make than it looks, provided you mark the sawing depth with tape and control the splits. The tapered-joint mallet draws on reaming skills used for the leg joints in the Raised Ax Block project; *see* p56.

SPLIT-LOG MALLET

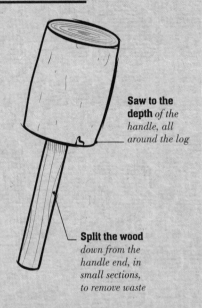

Saw to the depth *of the handle, all around the log*

Split the wood *down from the handle end, in small sections, to remove waste*

TAPERED-JOINT MALLET

Flared end *fits securely in tapered hole*

Drilled hole *is reamed to a taper*

Metal bands *to help hold together the wood fibers*

MAKE A
RAISED AX BLOCK

This is an essential axwork tool for the remaining projects in the book, and fitting the legs gives you a simple introduction to joinery, since tapered tenons are strong but forgiving of minor inaccuracies. When using, adopt a wide stance, with the leg on your dominant side a step back, so that it isn't in the way if you accidentally swing the ax through.

YOU WILL NEED

TOOLS AND EQUIPMENT

- Ax
- Mallet
- Wedges
- Pencil and compass
- Auger 1in (25mm) in diameter
- Protractor
- Sliding bevel
- Tape
- Straight knife

MATERIALS

- 1 log of green wood, about 5⅞in (150mm) in diameter and 30in (760mm) in length, for the legs

- 1 log of green or dry wood, about 12in (305mm) in diameter and 17in (430mm) deep, for the block; a softer wood is easier to carve, but if the block will be kept outside you may want a more durable wood and/or one with more tannin, to slow the rot

SKILLS

YOU WILL LEARN TO

- Split a log with an ax and wedges: *steps 1–3*
- Form a tapered tenon joint: *steps 5–12*
- Drill angled holes: *step 8*
- Ream with a knife: *step 9*

REMIND YOURSELF HOW TO

- Shape with an ax: *p50*
- Use an auger: *p30*

KNIFE GRIPS

- Thumb pull: *p21*
- Chest lever: *p19*
- Shin pull: *p63*

DESIGN GUIDE

The top of the block should be about waist height. There is enough mass in the block to cope with the impact from the ax without vibrating too much. The legs are wide apart for stability without being constant trip hazards, and can be removed for easy storage.

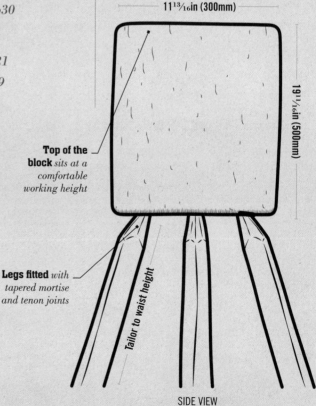

11¹³⁄₁₆in (300mm)

19¹¹⁄₁₆in (500mm)

Top of the block *sits at a comfortable working height*

Legs fitted *with tapered mortise and tenon joints*

Tailor to waist height

SIDE VIEW

"FOR THE **FREQUENT** WOODCRAFTER, AXING AT **WAIST HEIGHT** IS GOOD FOR AVOIDING **BACK STRAIN.**"

TIP
When you start chasing the split, hold the ax to prevent it from falling out, and to help keep the log stable.

" CAREFULLY **AX** APART ANY **FIBERS** STILL **ATTACHED**, **WATCHING** WHERE THE **SWING** MAY **FOLLOW THROUGH.** "

The Process

1 Start the split
Take the longer log and rest it against the fat log that will form the block piece. Position the blade of the ax across the center of a cut end and give the ax head a few solid taps with the mallet, until the blade is submerged and the wood is beginning to split down the fibers.

2 Chase the split
With the ax still embedded, rest the log horizontally and, gripping the handle of the ax, tap in the first wedge close to the limit of the split. Knock in a second wedge to continue the split. This will loosen the first wedge, which you can then knock in beyond the second wedge. Continue chasing the split until the log is cloven in two.

Hold the ax *straight upright and centered*

Start shaving *just beyond midpoint and flip to work the other half*

3 Split each half again

Rest one of the log halves flat side-down on the ax block and split it in half again. Use the same method, but make the initial split with the ax at the midpoint of the log. As the wood gets thinner the risk of running off increases (*see* p18), and by splitting from the middle you are effectively halving this risk. Repeat with the other log half, and then pick the three best log pieces, most evenly matched in girth, for the legs. As an alternative to this technique you could use a cleaving brake and froe; *see* p130.

4 Dress the leg

Work over a leg piece with the ax, removing the outer and inner bark, which make the wood more prone to rotting, and smoothing the surface; keep your supporting hand far away from the chopping action. The raised ax block will be "flat-packable" and the legs will be handled frequently, so it is important to remove any splinters and sharp edges. Don't chop away too much wood, though, to maintain leg strength.

Technique: Shaping with an ax—see p50

CONTINUED ☛

FOCUS ON...
TAPERED TENON JOINT

Since a tapered joint relies upon accuracy of the taper gradient rather than sizing, slight discrepancies don't affect fit, and when the tenon shrinks, it simply moves further into the mortise. It is also great for flat-packing, since it can be freed from a tight fit with a simple tap, whereas a straight tenon must be forced out along its whole length.

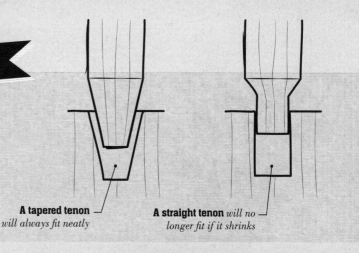

A tapered tenon *will always fit neatly*

A straight tenon *will no longer fit if it shrinks*

5 Mark the tenon width
Pick the straighter end of the dressed leg for the tapered tenon. Mark the minimum width with a circle 1in (25mm) in diameter, positioned roughly in the middle of the end face. A good way to do this is by screwing in the auger a little bit to leave a dimple.

Position roughly *in the middle of the end face*

6 Cut the taper
Ax the tenon to shape, starting from about 2¹⁵⁄₁₆in (75mm) up the leg, until it has tapered down close to the correct diameter with a small amount of waste. Keep checking the end as you cut, to see if you are nearing the guideline. Alternatively, a draw knife and shaving horse are useful for shaping the tenon, since you can see the diameter guide as you shave; *see* p94. Repeat steps 4–6 to make the other legs.

DRILLING ANGLED HOLES

Keep the auger aligned in two planes as you drill: straight forward on the sightline and at angle of splay.

For a tripod like this the sightlines dissect the other two holes, so that the feet of the legs will match the same equilateral triangle, only bigger; here we have marked one sightline in chalk for clarity.

Line up the sliding bevel with the splay angle parallel with the sightline. Get someone else to sight, or check the bevel alignment after every few turns of the auger.

7 Mark the leg positions
Determine the position of the legs on the underside of the block. Figure out the spacing by marking an equilateral triangle (all internal angles 60°) on the block face. The triangle should be centered, and of a size so that the legs are neither too close together, nor too near the edge of the block, and avoid any splits in the log.

Mark *the leg positions with chalk*

8 Start the mortise holes
Set the angle of splay for the legs. An angle of 30° from the vertical usually works well, but test by holding the legs in place to see if it looks good and is practical. Use a protractor to set the angle on a sliding bevel. Cut the initial holes for the legs by drilling in the auger at the angle of the bevel and to a depth of $2^{15}/_{16}$in (75mm). It is vital to maintain correct alignment as you drill; *see* Cutting angled holes, above.

Mark *the drilling depth with tape to act as a guide*

CONTINUED ☞

FOCUS ON...
REAMING THE HOLES

Reaming can be done with a specialized drill attachment called a reamer, which is the most accurate way of doing it. When reaming with a knife, it is easiest going into the end grain, and much more difficult if the grain runs horizontally through the hole. Always keep the tip of the knife in the hole so that it does not slip out.

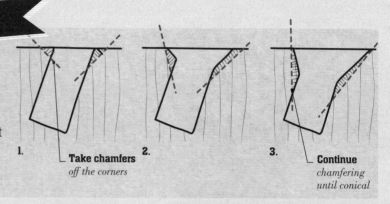

1. **Take chamfers** *off the corners*

2.

3. **Continue** *chamfering until conical*

Ⓖ Ream the mortise holes

Use a knife to cut sloping sides to the mortise holes so that they mirror the conical tenons; called "reaming." Widen each hole to 1⅜in (35mm) in diameter and mark the additional width to remove. Cut a chamfer to this line, then cut deeper in by successively taking off the corners of this initial chamfer; *see* Reaming the holes, above. When making twisting cuts, it can help to use your other hand to support and act as a pivot point, for more control. Always keep the tip of the knife in the hole so there's no risk of it slipping out.

10 Shave tenons

Make final shaping cuts to the leg tenons so that they fit the mortises. Be sure you have enough wood for the widest point of the reamed hole; the depth of the hole lets you know where that thickness is needed on the tenon. First cut a chamfer at the end to the circle guideline, using thumb pull grip. Switch to chest lever grip to shave off the waste left from the initial shaping. If your supporting arm gets tired, use shin pull grip so you can rest the leg on your thigh; *see* above right.

Knife grips: Thumb pull, chest lever—see pp21, 19

Lock the knife into position between your shin and knee, with the back of the blade resting against your leg.

To effect the cut hold the knife still and draw the wood back toward you.

Hold the edge of the blade at an angle and draw the wood diagonally across it.

Design variations

The basic block can be adapted to give upright surfaces for additional support in the chopping area. And fitting shorter legs to a halved log makes an easy, rough-and-ready bench.

BENCH

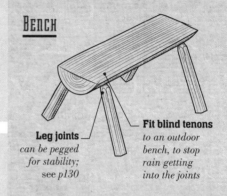

Leg joints *can be pegged for stability; see p130*

Fit blind tenons *to an outdoor bench, to stop rain getting into the joints*

BACKED BLOCK

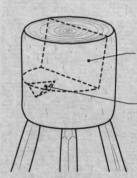

Saw out *a segment of the block to create a back for supporting billets*

Cut a notch *for shaping objects like spoons, so that the handles can dangle securely*

PEGGED BLOCK

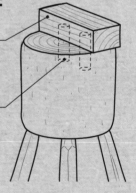

Wooden block *fitted as a back support*

Peg the block *by inserting dowels into drilled holes*

11 Test the fit

As you shave the tenons, keep testing the fit by knocking the leg firmly into its mortise. Look for telltale scuff marks on the tenon, which indicate where the tenon is slightly too big and causing friction. Shave off these raised areas with the knife. Note that if you increase the angle of taper for a better fit, you may need to start the taper farther back on the leg to maintain a straight line. If you struggle to get the legs out, tap them on the sides with the mallet: the vibrations have a loosening effect.

Scuff marks *on the tenon reveal where material must be removed*

MAKE A
COAT PEG

Over millions of years, trees have evolved the shape and grain orientation of side branches to build in great strength at the join. It's difficult to think of another green wood artifact that takes a lighter touch with what nature already has to offer.

YOU WILL NEED

TOOLS & EQUIPMENT
- Ax block
- Ax
- Handsaw (such as a pull saw)
- Drill and ⅛in (3mm) drill bit
- Straight knife
- *optional:* Plywood scrap

MATERIALS
- A forked branch section, about 9¹⁄₁₆in (230mm) long and 1in (25mm) diameter; it is usually best when the secondary branch has a slightly narrower diameter
- ⅛ x 1⁹⁄₁₆in (6 x 40mm) screws

SKILLS

YOU WILL LEARN TO
- Make a square countersink: *steps 6–7*

REMIND YOURSELF HOW TO
- Use an electric drill: *p24*
- Cut a chamfered finish: *p16*

KNIFE GRIPS
- Chest lever: *p19*
- Thumb pull: *p21*
- Thumb pivot: *p22*

DESIGN GUIDE

The main considerations of the design involve the practicalities of attaching the peg: a flat back; screw points that don't spoil the appearance; and a hook length that allows access for a screwdriver.

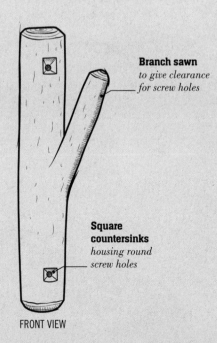

Chamfered finish *to all three ends*

An offset branch *makes the perfect natural hook*

Flat side *for attaching to wall or other surface*

Branch sawn *to give clearance for screw holes*

Square countersinks *housing round screw holes*

SIDE VIEW

FRONT VIEW

66 FOR A STRONG PEG YOU WANT A NICE, WIDE SURFACE AGAINST THE WALL. **99**

TIP
The secondary branch is less prone to splitting, as it is held together by the primary branch.

The Process

1 Flatten the back
Rest the wood on the block and use an ax to chop and shave a flat surface to the side opposite the offset branch. Chop until you get just beyond the pith; when left in the round, wood tends to split, so by removing slightly more than half of the wood you are creating a stronger, semicylindrical shape.

Chop to the middle *then flip it around to shave the other half*

2 Trim the side branch
The length of the hook should be long enough to be functional, but not so long that you do not have room to insert the top screw. Saw off as much of the side branch as is needed to give clearance for a screwdriver, using a pull saw or other type of handsaw. Hold the blade raised up at an angle to avoid catching the main branch, but cut straight across.

Technique: Using a pull saw—see p24

Guide the blade *with the thumb or finger of your supporting hand*

3 Drill screw holes

Position the drill at the center point of your piece of wood, about 1in (25mm) from the top, and drill straight down all the way through. If you find the drill is running off target, you can usually correct this by angling the drill for the first couple of seconds so the drill bit can fit comfortably in the groove you have made, then adjusting your angle so you are drilling straight downward. Drill another hole in the same position at the opposite end of the coat peg.

Technique: Using an electric drill—see p24

4 Shave the back

Refine the rough axed surface of the back of the peg with a knife in chest lever grip, making it as flat and smooth as you can. Complete one half first, before flipping the peg around to work down the other half. You are essentially repeating the actions you took in step 1 with the ax, but to a more refined finish.

Knife grip: Chest lever— see p19

Check that the wood *is flat by holding it against the wall or another flat surface*

CONTINUED ☞

5 Chamfer the ends

Use the thumb pull grip to cut chamfers around the three end points of the peg, and shave off any sawn surfaces, to give your coat peg a neater finish. At this point, if you prefer a less rustic look, you could remove all of the bark or even carve the surface to create a more refined design.

Technique: Cutting a chamfered finish—see p16

Knife grip: Thumb pull—see p21

— Don't chamfer
the edges *that
need to sit
flush against
the wall*

6 Start the countersink

Rest your cutting arm on the ax block so it doesn't slip. Hold the peg flat on the block with one hand, and hold the knife in the other; your knife hand should be in a fist with the blade facing away from you. Without removing any wood, make four incisions, each about 1/16in (2mm) or so in length, at the corner points of the hole.

— Use your arm
*as a pivot to
guide the knife*

> **" CARVING A SQUARE COUNTERSINK** AROUND THE SCREW HOLES NOT ONLY **LOOKS GOOD,** IT IS ALSO **EASIER** THAN CARVING A **ROUND** COUNTERSINK. **"**

7 Cut the countersink

Using the thumb pivot grip, cut out the sections between the points of the cross to form a square. Resting your hand on the block gives you more control, so you don't slip with the tip of the knife. Rest the end of the peg on the block and pivot it as you cut. Cut diagonally down into the hole with the tip of the knife, then remove each section of the countersink bit by bit. Repeat steps 6–7 on the other hole.

Knife grip: Thumb pivot— see p22

8 Let the peg dry

If using very green wood, screw your coat peg onto a scrap of plywood to keep it straight while it dries. This method is also useful if you are making several pegs and don't intend to put them up right away. It is also advisable to spread some wood glue on the exposed end grain of the secondary branch, to protect it against splitting.

Design variations

Depending on the size and shape of your branch, you can create a range of handy objects for use in your hallway or around your home using branches like this one. For instance, two of these coat pegs could be used to hold up a curtain rod.

MULTI-HOOK

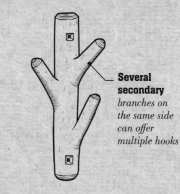

Several secondary *branches on the same side can offer multiple hooks*

COAT STAND

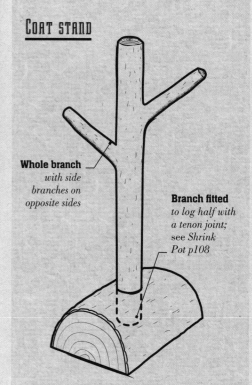

Whole branch *with side branches on opposite sides*

Branch fitted *to log half with a tenon joint; see Shrink Pot p108*

MAKE A
COOKING SPOON

A spoon is one of the first tools we ever use as babies, and the simple appearance belies a surprisingly complex design that takes practice to get right. With this project you will learn how to carve a hollow in the bowl of a spoon and shape the convex back of the bowl into the neck.

YOU WILL NEED

EQUIPMENT
- Ax, ax block, and mallet
- Straight knife
- Spoon knife

MATERIALS
- 1 log of green wood, about $4^{15}/_{16}$in (125mm) in diameter and $7^{7}/_{8}$in (200mm) in length

SKILLS

YOU WILL LEARN TO
- Carve a bowl shape: *steps 2–3, 8, 13–15*
- Use a bent knife: *steps 16–19*

REMIND YOURSELF HOW TO
- Split with an ax: *p56*
- Shape with an ax: *p50*
- Cut a chamfered finish: *p16*

KNIFE GRIPS
- Reinforced pull: *p32*
- Thumb pivot: *p22*
- Chest lever: *p19*
- Thumb pull: *p21*
- Thumb push: *p22*
- Shin pull: *p63*

DESIGN GUIDE

The relatively thick, blunt rim of the bowl is designed to protect the spoon from the daily wear and tear of cooking. A wide handle with a rounded end is comfortable for gripping as you vigorously stir food in a pan. The hollow is fairly shallow, as this spoon is intended for stirring rather than scooping. For the order and direction of cuts, refer to the diagrams on pp77 and 80.

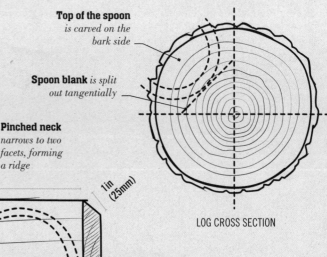

Top of the spoon *is carved on the bark side*

Spoon blank *is split out tangentially*

LOG CROSS SECTION

Handle facets *finish with a chamfered end for comfort*

Pinched neck *narrows to two facets, forming a ridge*

$7^{7}/_{8}$in (200mm)

1in (25mm)

$2^{1}/_{2}$in (65mm)

Peaked edge *for scraping the bottom of pots*

OVERHEAD VIEW

" OUT OF THE BLANK, WITH JUST A FEW CHOPS AND SHAVES OF THE AX, THE RUDIMENTARY SHAPE OF A SPOON QUICKLY BEGINS TO FORM. **"**

The Process

1 Split out a blank

Split out a quarter log and shave to around ³⁄₁₆in (5mm) wider than the finished spoon; if very wide, chop or cleave further to quickly reduce the size. Take the peak off the back, removing at least the pith and the first couple of growth rings.

Techniques: Splitting with an ax, shaping with an ax—see pp56, 50

The bark *side will form the top of the spoon*

Cut long *shavings from the middle*

2 Facet the back

Working on the non-bark side of the blank, begin to shape the back of the bowl of the spoon by chopping two facets down the corner edges of each side. You want to end up with three equal-sized facets across the back, and two square edges on the sides. For safety, and to control your cuts, always chop from the middle, flipping the blank around to chop the other way.

Make angled *chops to split the fibers*

⅃ Start to shape handle

Chop out some of the side bulk, taking waste from just below the start of the bowl. When carving into the neck at the top of the handle, be very careful not to cut your spoon supporting hand. You shouldn't be swinging with your arm at this stage, instead use very controlled flicks of the ax, making sure not to lift the ax high enough that it could come down on to your supporting hand

⅃ Round the bowl forward

Round the bowl on a second plane by chopping two facets forward, from just beyond the middle of the bowl to the front edge. Create these curves by executing "bump cuts:" place the ax where you want to make the cut; tilt it until you feel the edge bite into the wood; then lift together both ax and blank, and "bump" them down on the block to effect the cut. Change the angle slightly with each bump cut to create a rough dome shape.

"Bump cut" *right to the front edge of what will be the bowl*

CONTINUED ☞

TIP

If you don't create a break in the fibers before shaping the crank, there's a risk you will split off the entire top of the bowl.

Keep the cuts *close together and chop out the waste*

Take off the **corners** *either side of the central cut*

5 Relieve the crank

The next stage is to shape the crank of the spoon, which is the slope between the handle and the bowl. Before shaping, however, you need to you need to break up the fibers where the lowest point of the crank will be, by making a series of shallow chops straight across the center of the bowl.

6 Angle the crank

Starting on the handle side, chop diagonally down from where you want to begin the neck into the first part of the bowl. The tip of the ax does most of the work and shouldn't go beyond the initial vertical cuts made in the previous step.

> **THE AX IS A TOOL UNIQUELY SUITED TO SHAPING IN THREE DIMENSIONS, BUT IT MUST BE USED CAREFULLY!**

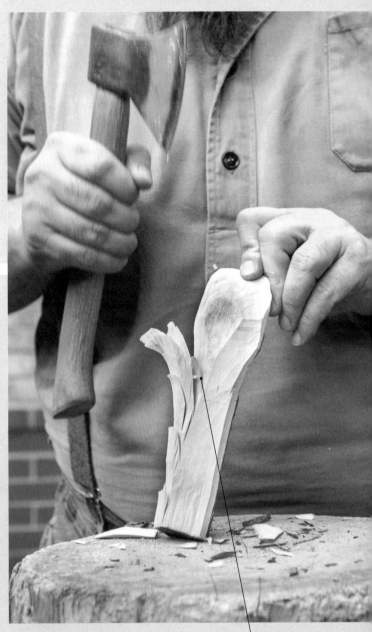

7 Complete the crank
Turn the blank around and make similar sloping cuts from the bowl side, back toward the center of the bowl.

— **Chop on the edge** *of the block to stop the ax*

8 Rough shape the handle
Chop out most of the waste from the back of the handle, still following the facets set in step 2. Remove the outer and inner bark from the top side. Then remove most of the bulk from the back of the handle; in particular, remove waste at the back shoulders and take cuts into the neck.

— **Side facets** *should curve in at the neck*

CONTINUED ☞

" AS YOU FACET THE RIM, FEEL FOR WHEN
THE GRAIN CHANGES DIRECTION,
THEN FLIP THE SPOON AND PUSH THE BLADE
THE OTHER WAY. "

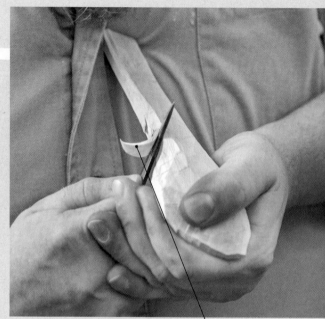

9 Dress the bowl

Switching to knifework, refine the top surface of the bowl with reinforced pull grip, working your way from the rim back toward the neck; notice the thumb tucked safely behind the spoon. You should be able to take shavings all the way into the neck by angling the blade, but you may need to come back down the handle toward the bowl, using thumb pivot grip.

Knife grips: Reinforced pull, Thumb pivot—see pp32, 22

10 Refine the neck

Return to reinforced pull strokes to continue to shape the neck. Neaten up the ax cuts and create a narrower shape to the neck by taking cuts in tighter from both sides, as well as from the top and bottom.

Start cuts *at the bowl and continue down the handle*

This diagram offers a guide to the direction of shaping cuts required at the back of the spoon, and the best grips to effect them. The trickiest part to carve is the shoulder of the bowl and into the neck, where you are shaping on several planes to form the sweeping convex and ridge.

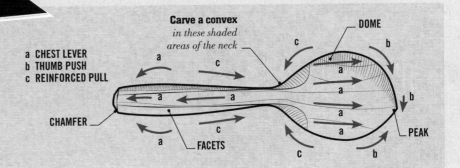

a CHEST LEVER
b THUMB PUSH
c REINFORCED PULL

Carve a convex *in these shaded areas of the neck*

DOME

CHAMFER

FACETS

PEAK

You can use *your supporting hand's thumb to steady the initial cut*

11 Dome the bowl

Switch to chest lever grip to cut a dome shape to the back of the bowl of the spoon. Refine the convex shape begun with the axwork by cutting multiple short facets. Cut in the direction of the bowl rim, remembering to bring the top of the rim to an asymmetrical peak.

Knife grip: Chest lever—see p19

12 Neaten the back

Cut a square facet around the rim of the bowl using thumb push grip. Blend a convex curve into the neck with reinforced pull. Then refine the handle facets with chest lever, switching to shin pull grip if you start to get tired.

Knife grips: Thumb push, shin pull —see pp22, 63

Smooth the surface *by taking long, thin shavings*

CONTINUED ☞

TIP

When cutting the neck, you can press the fingers of your reinforcing hand on the back of the blade to help direct it.

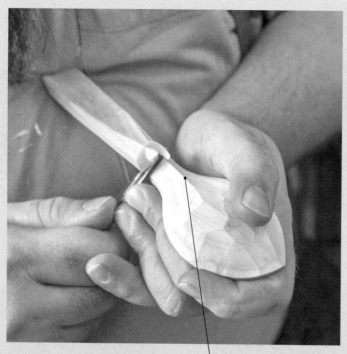

Start the
ridge *from
the shoulder
of the dome*

13 Pinch in the neck

Remove more material from the neck, making cuts with reinforced pull. Take shavings from all sides, but try not to lose too much depth: you are aiming to pinch in the neck to a keellike narrow ridge where it joins the bowl, which gradually widens out to three broad facets down the length of the handle.

14 Shape and chamfer the handle

Finish shaping the handle with chest lever grip, flaring it out before tapering it back in slightly toward the end. Dress the handle with long, thin shavings for a smooth finish. Cut a chamfer into the end of the handle using thumb pull grip; chamfering gives a neat finish, prevents fibers from furring, and makes the spoon comfortable to hold.

Technique: Cutting a chamfered finish—see p16

Knife grip: Thumb pull—see p21

When carving a curve, there is a midpoint beyond which, if you keep cutting, the blade will catch on the ends of the fibers and tear into the wood. This is why we say to carve down hill to the bottom of the valley.

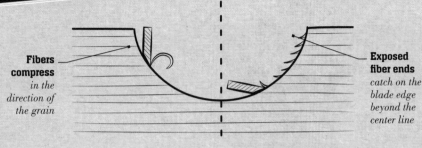

Fibers compress *in the direction of the grain*

Exposed fiber ends *catch on the blade edge beyond the center line*

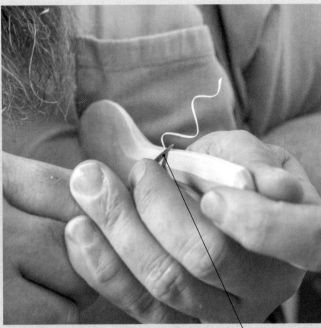

Continuous *shavings give a smooth finish*

15 Finish the edges

Returning to reinforced pull, cut the corners off all edges to remove any sharp points and refine the finish. Cut a wide facet into the edge on the front of the bowl, along the side that culminates in the offset peak, which will form the scraping area of the spoon. Use thumb push to cut this facet.

16 Hollow the bowl

Draw a pencil guideline to set the extent of the hollow, leaving a fairly wide rim. Use a bent knife for hollowing out; *see* p81. Take small shavings initially, and start on the far side of the bowl, which is more difficult to cut since the guiding bevel of the blade has less wood to rest on. Use the thumb pull grip as shown, with your thumb safe behind the spoon and supported on your leg so it doesn't slip. Cut directly across the grain and build up the length of shavings to reach the far side of the spoon.

Manually guide *the edge of the blade into the cut, on the far side*

CONTINUED ☞

FOCUS ON...

CUTS TO THE TOP

Hollowing out the bowl is the main challenge when carving the top, requiring several changes of grip. When shaping the curves, aim to think in quadrants to avoid digging into the grain; *see* Cutting to the center, p79.

a THUMB PULL
b REINFORCED PULL
c THUMB PUSH with edge reversed
d THUMB PUSH
e CHEST LEVER

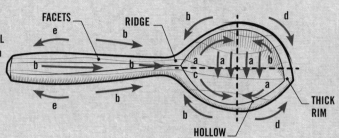

FACETS   RIDGE   THICK RIM   HOLLOW

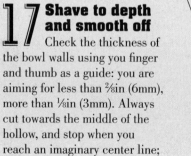

Follow the curve *but don't cross the center line*

17 Shave to depth and smooth off

Check the thickness of the bowl walls using you finger and thumb as a guide: you are aiming for less than ⅜in (6mm), more than ⅛in (3mm). Always cut towards the middle of the hollow, and stop when you reach an imaginary center line; *see* Cutting to the center, p79. Build up to longer shavings, which will take the bowl deeper. Once you've reached the right depth, smooth the surface with sweeping shaves.

18 Employ the reversed thumb push

Chasing a shaving around the quadrant's rim can be tricky with other grips. Come at it instead with a variation of thumb pivot grip, whereby the blade is reversed from its usual position and you push the blade edge across the grain.

A spoon knife has a convex curving blade, which allows it to cut smoothly on the concave surface of a hollow.

Make cuts using the same grips as with a straight knife, and following the same safety tips, such as here keeping the thumb tucked behind in thumb pull grip.

Design variations

The shape of the bowl is a good place to start experimenting. An oval or circular shape with a thin rim is right for an eating spoon, while tapering tips and squarer sides are good for scraping, stirring, and serving.

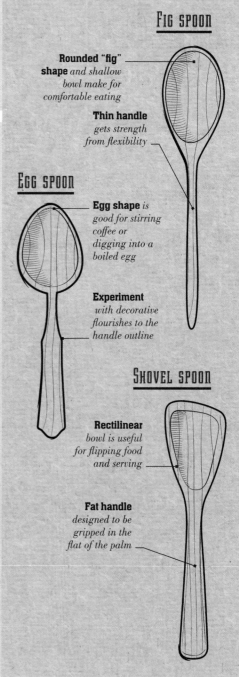

FIG SPOON

Rounded "fig" shape *and shallow bowl make for comfortable eating*

Thin handle *gets strength from flexibility*

EGG SPOON

Egg shape *is good for stirring coffee or digging into a boiled egg*

Experiment *with decorative flourishes to the handle outline*

SHOVEL SPOON

Rectilinear *bowl is useful for flipping food and serving*

Fat handle *designed to be gripped in the flat of the palm*

19 Smooth out the grooves

Hollowing out the bowl leaves small grooves on the rim. Smooth these off by cutting wide shavings around the inner edge. You will need to use different grips to get at all four quadrants of the rim: thumb pull, reinforced pull, and thumb push with the edge of the blade reversed.

Remove the *corners of the rim and the pencil lines*

MAKE A
BOWL

This elegant bowl incorporates handles and a relatively shallow and elongated hollow, making it perfect for serving food. You will learn to work with an adze and bowl gouge, and gain insights into coping with the changing direction of grain when chopping out and carving a hollow form.

YOU WILL NEED

TOOLS & EQUIPMENT
- Mallet and froe
- Ax and ax block
- Pencil and measuring equipment
- Workbench with upright supports and wedges
- Adze or gouge with metal end to handle and small mallet
- Bowl gouge
- Hook knife, scorper, or dogleg gouge
- Push knife
- Handsaw (such as a pull saw)
- Straight knife
- *optional:* Draw knife, holdfast

MATERIALS
- A green wood log, about 9¹³⁄₁₆in (250mm) in diameter and 14³⁄₁₆in (360mm) in length

SKILLS

YOU WILL LEARN TO
- Split with a froe: *steps 1–3*
- Use an adze: *steps 8–9, 11*
- Measure thickness: *step 10*
- Use a bowl gouge: *step 12*
- Use a push knife: *step 17*

REMIND YOURSELF HOW TO
- Shape with an ax: *p50*
- Use a draw knife: *p94*
- Use a hook knife: *p70*
- Use a pull saw: *p24*

KNIFE GRIPS
- Spoon knife: *p74*
- Thumb push: *p22*
- Thumb pull: *p21*

DESIGN GUIDE

The diameter of the log largely determines the type of bowl that can be carved. The size we used is big enough for a large eating bowl. A wider log would be needed for a salad or fruit bowl, and narrower log for a small eating bowl or cup.

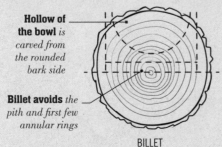

Hollow of the bowl *is carved from the rounded bark side*

Billet avoids *the pith and first few annular rings*

BILLET

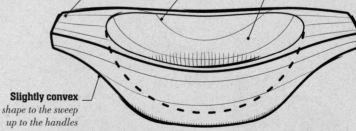

Rim expands *to form handles at the narrower ends of the hollow*

Rim dips *and rises along the sides of the hollow*

Aim for *a thickness of ⅜in (10mm) to the nonhandle areas of the bowl*

Slightly convex *shape to the sweep up to the handles*

SIDE VIEW

" HANDLES LEND VERSATILITY, AS WELL AS ADDING **STRENGTH** TO THE SHORT END **GRAIN.** "

❝ IT IS IMPORTANT TO ACHIEVE A

SMOOTH, FLAT SURFACE TO

THE BASE SIDE, FOR JUDGING THE

DEPTH OF THE BOWL. **❞**

The Process

Some fibers *may remain attached and can be severed with an ax*

1 Start the first split

To form the billet, place the log on an ax block and line up the blade of the froe across the center of the log. For the first hit, keep the arm holding the froe relaxed to avoid moving the blade as you hit it, and tap gently with the mallet. Once the blade has made the initial cut, give it a few more forceful knocks until it is fully submerged.

2 Chase the split

Now use the handle as a lever, pulling and pushing to chase the split down right through. Choose a half and draw guidelines for your billet, indicating where to make splits. Take the wood from above the pith and first few rings, and form a billet with three straight sides and a curved top, centered on the apex; ours was about 7⅞in (200mm) wide and 4½in (115mm) deep. Split away the sides; the splits may run off as they are near the edge, but you can correct this with an ax.

Your body *provides opposing force for the levering action with the froe*

Keep the fingers *of your supporting hand far away from the chopping action*

The blade *should be submerged in the wood*

3 Split out the billet

Next, split off the first couple of growth rings and pith. Still resting the log on the ax block, position the froe on the guideline, knock it in, then move to the floor to kneel on the log as you lever the split.

4 True the sides

Refine the split surfaces with the ax. You are making them straight and smooth so that the billet will clamp to the workbench, and so you can be confident of the dimensions of the bowl. Resting the billet on the ax block, chop and shave with the ax to true the sides so that they are parallel. For a neater finish, keep the ax head more vertical and make skewed cuts.

Technique: Shaping with an ax—see p50

CONTINUED ☛

Take progressively *less material off each facet as you approach the final line of your curve*

Hold diagonally, *lean in with elbows locked, and pull with your whole body, leading from your strong arm*

5 Assess and true the curve

Roughly remove the outer bark to assess the curve of the billet. You are checking for trueness: is it wonky, raised on one side? Work facets around the curved surface, aiming to make the curve more shallow by taking most material from the middle facet. Once hollowed, this shape creates a new sweeping curve along the bowl as seen from the side.

6 Shave with a draw knife

If you have one, a draw knife will achieve a more consistent line to the top curve and a near-final smooth finish. A draw knife allows greater control because you make cuts toward your body and can use the resistance of your body to control the blade. By contrast, with an ax you are pushing the blade away from your body and resistance is coming from the billet.

Technique: Using a draw knife—see p94

Employ a swinging action with the adze to chop out wood, keeping your body out of the line of the swing. Support your wrist with your other hand for greater control.

Strike the wood at an angle of about 30° to remove thick chips; too perpendicular and the blade won't penetrate, too shallow and it will only skim the surface.

To make more accurate shavings, turn the blade edge more to the horizontal, so the outside bevel rubs the wood, guiding the cut, and employ gentler strokes.

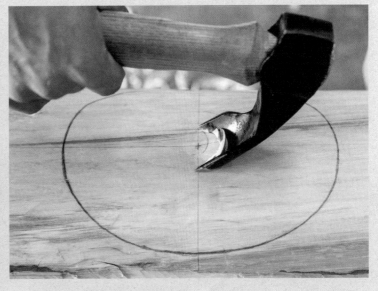

7 Draw the hollow

Curved surface facing up, mark the center point of the billet, then lines dividing it into quadrants. The longer line should ideally be straight and central, but needs to follow the direction of the grain; this shouldn't be a problem if you have trued the sides correctly. Draw the shape of the hollow of the bowl, keeping the center point in the middle.

Wedging the billet between uprights is one way to secure it

8 Start chopping out the hollow

Chop out an initial dimple from the center of the hollow, using a curved adze (*see* above). This first dimple gives clearance for chips which would otherwise have nowhere to split off into. Chop out from this starting point, removing about 1in (25mm) of material at a time, steadily expanding downward and out toward the rim line but stopping slightly short.

CONTINUED ☞

CUTTING OUT A HOLLOW

A hollow form must be excavated little by little, always working from the rim to the center but not beyond. Most chips will come from the center of the bowl, but accurately cutting into the end grain is the hard work. For the first cut on the rim, it is best to aim for the inside of the rim and then adjust until your cuts are hitting accurately.

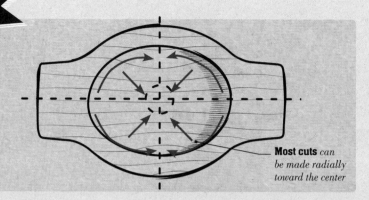

Most cuts *can be made radially toward the center*

9 Expand the hollow

Once you have hollowed out to the initial depth, return to the center and go deeper. Always chop toward the center of the billet, going with the grain. If need be, stop chopping and remove loose chips so you can see what you're doing. A good practice is to chop out quadrant by quadrant, but it is not necessary to follow such a sequence. Continue chopping out the hollow until you think you are approaching a suitable depth.

Use large, *confident chops for relatively smooth facets*

10 Check base thickness

Measure the depth of the hollow to check the thickness of the base; a good thickness to aim for is ⅜–½in (10–12mm). You can try measuring with your finger and thumb, which are surprisingly accurate gauges of depth. For greater accuracy, take two rulers—or a ruler and anything else flat and straight—rest one on the rim and measure down with the other, then transfer this measurement to the side of the bowl.

Using a Bowl Gouge

Adopt a wide stance as if lunging forwards, with the leg on your weaker side foremost.

Grip with the handle end pressed into your palm, line up your forearm with the blade, and tuck in your elbow.

Push gently by bracing the gouge against your body and using your bodyweight for force.

Guide the blade with your weaker arm, ensuring the bevel is in contact with the wood to direct the edge. Keep your steadying arm resting on the billet or bench.

11 Start refining the surface

Employ "shaving mode" with the adze to cut an accurate line around the top edge, almost up to the line of the bowl rim. The blade edge of the adze should be closer to the horizontal for shallower cuts that take off less wood in thinner chips. Remember, you are still cutting only as far as the center and then changing direction. Once you have a neat edge around the rim, you can use more forceful cuts to even out the rest of the hollow. Do not get carried away trying to create a perfect finish at this point, though—you will do that with a gouge.

12 Refine with the gouge

Switch to using a bowl gouge to create a smoother finish (*see above*). Take off the corner of the rim with a thin chamfer. Work carefully: the more you can create the rim shape with a single cut to each quadrant, the neater the finish. Then dress the surface of the rest of the hollow, making refinements to the shape and aiming to get rid of marks left by the adze for a smooth finish; you can peel off wider shavings at this stage.

Don't be nervous *gripping fairly close to the blade edge: the direction of the cut is away from your hand*

TIP
Keep the handle of the bowl knife as low as possible to engage the shallower section of the curved blade.

❝ TO MAKE ACCURATE SHAPING CUTS WITH AN AX, MOVE YOUR HAND NEARER TO THE AX HEAD AND SWITCH TO SHORTER SWINGS AND WRIST FLICKS. **❞**

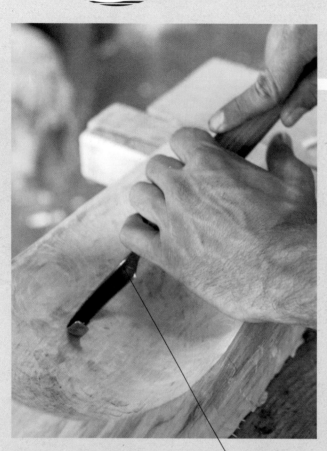

13 Refine the center of the hollow

You may struggle to reach all parts of the bowl with just one gouge. If you have problems getting into the curve at certain points in your bowl, switch to a tool with a tighter curve in the blade. For areas that regular, "stubbier" gouges cannot access—such as the tight space at the bottom of the hollow—you can use either a spoon knife, a scorper, or a dogleg gouge to smooth the surface.

Knife grip: Spoon knife—see p74

Rotate the blade *rather than pulling it toward you*

14 Draw the rim and dress the foot

Mark a guideline for the rim of the bowl, with a width of about ½in (12mm) at the thinnest point. Draw this outline parallel to the rim of the hollow, tapering it off to form the handles. Turn and reclamp the billet base up. Use the bowl gouge to carve a level surface and smooth finish to what will become the foot of the bowl. Gouge straight across the grain at a 90° angle. It is best to dress the surface of the foot at this stage, before shaping, when the bowl can still be easily clamped; it also helps with shaping by marking out the foot.

15 Shape the body

Remove waste with an ax, chopping in relief cuts then shaving down. Again, only work up to the midpoint, taking off the corners of one side then turning the bowl around to remove the opposite corners. Follow the shape of the hollow and keep feeling for thickness, taking care at the thinnest points around the central band—at this point the grain changes direction, so a misplaced ax swing could be disastrous. Hold the ax nearer the head when more accurate cuts are needed, and switch to a knife for sections that follow the grain.

A good process *for the shaping is to work five facets down the length of the bowl*

16 Shape the handles and refine

Once you're happy with the rounded sides, work the sweep up to the handle; it can be attractive to give each sweep a slightly concave profile. Leave some waste beyond the handle ends, as protection against the impact these surfaces receive from the axing and shaving, and so you don't have to worry about cutting the handles too short. Work over the whole surface again, removing large chop marks and ensuring a consistent shape and even thickness.

USING A PUSH KNIFE

Brace the piece to be worked with your body, securing it against an upright support on a workbench, or fix it in place with a block of scrap wood and a holdfast, if you have one.

Close your fists around both of the knife's handles to grip, and make cuts by pushing with the blade held on the diagonal.

A push knife has a short bevel to allow for concave cuts, so when working convex surfaces you need to avoid scooping in.

17 Shave a smooth finish

Finish the outside of the bowl with a push knife (*see above*), but leave a thin section around the rim untouched. Aim to cut a series of flat facets on the convex surfaces. As you move on to the sweep up to the handles, you can take more concave scoops; try to roll through in one motion to cut longer shavings. Alternatively, a draw knife, if you have one, makes quicker work of achieving a smooth finish.

18 Neaten the rim

Saw off most of the waste at the ends of the handles. Then use a knife and employ pull stroke to cut final crisp edges to the rim. If pull stroke becomes awkward as you move down the handles, switch to thumb pull grip. Dress the top surface to remove any rough patches and finger marks, using thumb push grip.

To avoid cutting *sections of rim base-side up, switch to thumb push grip*

Technique: Using a pull saw—see p24

Knife grips: Thumb pull, thumb push—see pp21, 22

Hold the bowl steady
and keep the thumb of your cutting hand safely tucked behind the bowl

19 Finish the handles

Chamfer each edge with thumb pull. Switch to thumb push to cut the handle curves, first chipping off pieces until you can blend the facets to a curve, then building up the curved end through a series of cuts from different angles. Return to pull stroke to peel off the sharp edge of the outer rim. Aim to remove the tiniest slither in a continuous shave. Do the same for the rim of the hollow, using either thumb pull or thumb push for different quadrants.

Design variations

Adding animal features is an ancient practice, and the sweeping form of a handle bowl suggests the shape of a bird. Bowls with steep, circular hollows have weaker structures, and these are best carved from wood with strong, interlocking grain: at a crook, from near the base of the tree, or from a burr.

BIRD BOWL

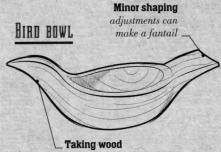

Minor shaping
adjustments can make a fantail

Taking wood
from the crook of a side branch can help form a raised head and tail

ROUND BOWL

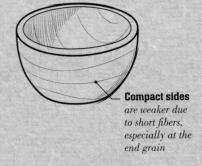

Compact sides
are weaker due to short fibers, especially at the end grain

CUP BOWL

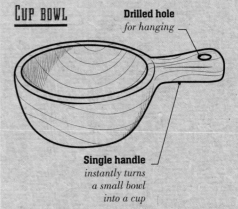

Drilled hole
for hanging

Single handle
instantly turns a small bowl into a cup

MAKE A
SERVING PLATTER

This simple platter is the perfect size for serving cheeses, presenting small cakes, or even using as an unconventional plate, and can double as a small chopping board. The project offers a good introduction to using a draw knife on a shaving horse, as well as practice at creating flat surfaces from cleft wood.

YOU WILL NEED

TOOLS & EQUIPMENT
- Mallet
- Froe
- Ax block
- Ax
- Pencil
- Shaving horse
- Draw knife
- Ruler
- Straight knife
- *optional*: Winding sticks

MATERIALS
- 1 green wood log, about 18⅞in (480mm) in length and 9¹³⁄₁₆in (250mm) in diameter

SKILLS

YOU WILL LEARN TO
- **Correct wind:** *steps 2–5*
- **True with an ax:** *step 3*
- **Use a draw knife:** *steps 7–10*

REMIND YOURSELF HOW TO
- **Split with a froe:** *p82*
- **Carve a chamfered edge:** *p16*

KNIFE GRIPS
- **Thumb pivot:** *p22*
- **Thumb pull:** *p21*
- **Chest lever:** *p19*
- **Reinforced pull:** *p32*

DESIGN GUIDE

The slim shape to the platter gives it elegance and is also practical, making it light enough to carry in one hand. The long, wide paddle also helps with gripping and balance.

4. ROUND CORNERS

18½in (470mm)

Handle starts *about a third of the way down*

3. CURVE HANDLES

4½in (115mm)

Edges of handle *are thickly chamfered*

Bottom corners *are rounded off*

¾in (29mm)

OVERHEAD VIEW

2. SHAVE SIDES

1. SHAVE FACES

"WOOD TAKEN FROM THE **RADIUS** OF A LOG **DOESN'T** HAVE **CURVED GROWTH RINGS** WITHIN IT, AND SO THE PLATTER **DRIES** WITH **MINIMAL CUPPING."**

CORRECTING WIND

Wood often splits with some kind of twist—or "wind"—in the grain. Winding sticks are simple tools to help you adjust for wind.

1. Place two straight sticks at either end of the billet and look across their top edges. The degree and points of misalignment indicate where to remove material to correct for wind.

2. Keep repositioning the sticks as you true the billet: once they align everywhere along the plank, the wind has been removed.

The Process

1 Split and square

Split out a quarter log. Halve the quarter, cutting in line with one of the straight sides, then split in half again for two thin billets. Use the one that lay along the radius, known as "quartersawn": when the growth rings are short and vertical through the plank, rather than long and curved and horizontal, you are less likely to get cupping in the cross section of the plank. With an ax, start to make the sides of the billet squarer.

Technique: Splitting with a froe—see p82

2 Rough shape the board

Draw on the shape of the handle at the more twisted end, if there is one. Holding the other end of the billet, take out the waste around the outline of the handle, while at the same time correcting for wind; *see* above. Much of the wind can be removed when shaping the handle. Keep sighting down your billet to identify thick areas that need shaving down. Shape one side of the handle first, then get the other side to match.

Mark on crosses *where there are thicker areas to chop down*

A draw knife is an effective tool for cutting along fibers and quickly taking off shavings for a smooth finish that's hard to achieve with an ax and straight knife.

Cuts are made by pulling with your whole body, holding the knife in both hands. This makes it much more powerful than a straight knife and allows you to work much faster.

You can only use a draw knife by pulling it toward you; if the grain dips down and the knife follows the grain, making it difficult to take a straight cut, it may be best to turn the billet around and work that part in the other direction.

4 Shape the handle and flatten the edges

Turn the board on its side to shape one of the curved sides of the handle and smooth down the edge, then turn it over and shape the other side in the same way. Start by slicing off the corners, then round them off by removing any sharp points, checking all the time to ensure the shape is even.

Start the parallel
line from the point of minimum width

3 Flatten the faces

Now use a draw knife to shave the surfaces of the platter flat and smooth; *see* above. Hold the knife on the diagonal, lock your elbows, and draw the blade toward you, pulling with your whole body. Shave one side of the board flat to create a datum surface, from which you can then flatten the other side by marking a parallel line along each edge.

CONTINUED ☞

TIP
Rounding the end prevents "spelching:" the splintering of fibers that occurs when wood is cut off across the grain.

Take care
around the unpredictable grain of knots

5 Chamfer sides
Use pull stroke, but without reinforcement, to cut a thin chamfer on each of the long edges. You must use a "stop" to avoid cutting yourself: draw your elbow back close to your body and, with the tip of the knife slightly away from you, use a "cocked" wrist so that the inside of your wrist hits your chest first. Even out surface rough patches, using thumb pivot to get into nooks and crannies.

Technique: Carving a chamfered edge—see p16

Knife grip: Thumb pivot—see p22

6 Round the ends
Shave the sawn surface smooth at the square end of the platter. First cut a wide chamfer along the edges with thumb pull grip, then switch to chest lever grip to cut between the chamfers; you may also find the reinforced pull grip useful for this step. Round off the corners by first cutting a bevel on the end, again with thumb pull grip.

Knife grips: Thumb pull, chest lever, reinforced pull— see pp21, 19, 32

> **CURVED** PROFILES ARE SHAPED **PROGRESSIVELY** BY KNOCKING OFF A SERIES OF **CORNERS** AND BLENDING IN THE **EDGES.**

Keep your thumb *behind the handle, out of harm's way*

7 Refine the handle

Cut a wide chamfer on the handle, continuing the three facets you cut into the square edges. Switch between thumb pull and thumb pivot, depending on the direction you need to cut. When shaping curves, for concaves remember to cut each "side of the valley" separately, stopping at the valley base to avoid cutting against the grain; for convexes, make separate cuts up each "side of the mountain." Push the board against your ax block to support it as you work.

Design variations

Drilling a hole into the handle allows a platter to be stored hanging up, but don't position it too close to the edge, to avoid weakness. Cutting a pair of asymmetrical platters is an economical use of a wider billet.

TWO-HANDLED PLATTER

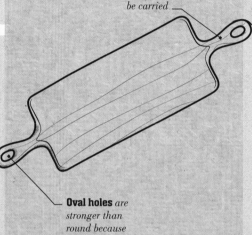

Handles at both ends *enable a longer board to be carried*

Oval holes *are stronger than round because they are narrow at the end grain*

ASYMMETRICAL PLATTERS

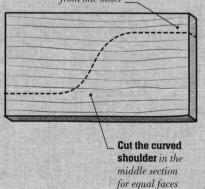

Placing the handle *at the side allows two platters to be cut from one billet*

Cut the curved shoulder *in the middle section for equal faces*

MAKE A
CUTTING BOARD

Planing a solid wood cutting board is a sensible project to complete before embarking on joinery, since it teaches you how to create completely flat and true surfaces from which accurate measurements may be taken. As a bonus, you will end up with a beautiful and useful item for the kitchen!

YOU WILL NEED

TOOLS & EQUIPMENT

- Pencil and ruler or measuring tape
- Work bench
- Bench stop
- Handsaw
- Scrub plane
- Winding sticks
- Jack plane
- Spare plywood
- Marking gauge
- Electric drill and ¼in (7mm) drill bit
- Frame saw
- Straight knife
- *optional*: F-clamp, vise, board gauge

MATERIALS

- Section of waney edge plank, avoiding end splits and areas of potential moisture damage
- Cardboard, for the handle template

SKILLS

YOU WILL LEARN TO

- Use planes: *steps 2–6, 8, 11*
- Measure from a datum: *steps 2–3, 5–8*
- Use a frame saw: *step 10*

REMIND YOURSELF HOW TO

- Correct wind: *p94*
- Use an electric drill: *p24*
- Cut a chamfered finish: *p16*

KNIFE GRIPS

- Thumb pivot: *p22*

DESIGN GUIDE

Aside from the practical elegance of the curved handle, the main design feature of the board lies in the tactile beauty of its planed surfaces.

Faces and sides *planed totally flat and straight to prevent rocking*

22⁷⁄₁₆in (570mm)

14³⁄₄in (375mm)

Handle for carrying *and hanging in the kitchen*

Handle cut out *with a frame saw and chamfered with a straight knife*

1³⁄₁₆in (30mm)

Straight sides *chamfered with a plane*

OVERHEAD VIEW

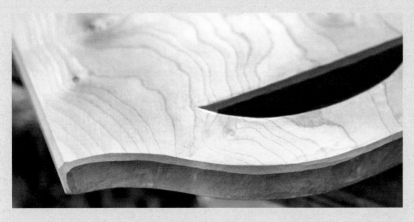

> **TREAT THE JOB OF PLANING AS A CHANCE TO DRAW OUT THE TREMENDOUS BEAUTY TO BE FOUND IN WOOD GRAIN.**

USING PLANES

Use your body to push behind your strongest arm with your other hand guiding. It is usually efficient to plane diagonally, overlapping cuts.

1. Scrub plane—Cuts thick shavings, useful for quickly roughing a flat surface. Maintain cuts in the same direction to take full length shavings.

2. Jack plane—This low-angled plane works well on end grain. An adjustable mouth can be reduced for the finest cuts. With its longer and wider sole it can be used for a "true" surface.

The Process

1 Rough cut to size

Mark and saw your boards roughly to size. For the greatest accuracy, sizing the boards will be done once the face has been planed flat. An edge is then accurately planed adjacent to it, and these two datum surfaces (face and edge) can be used for accurately marking out, something which is even more important for joinery projects.

Cut through *the central hole in your workbench, if it has one*

2 Select the datum side

If the board is very warped you may find that one side sits better on the work bench than the other. To hold the board in place, you can usually get away with just using a bench stop, but you may prefer to use an F-clamp as well. The first job is to rough the face with a scrub plane; note in the picture where the plane takes off the high points.

CUPPING

Planks are often cut tangentially out of logs—that is, not along the radius—and so tend to have the curved growth rings running horizontally through the plank. This can make planks prone to a type of warping called "cupping," caused by the annual growth rings attempting to flatten out as the wood dries.

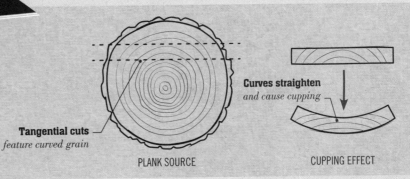

Tangential cuts
feature curved grain

PLANK SOURCE

Curves straighten
and cause cupping

CUPPING EFFECT

Plane the surface *until entirely flat and smooth*

⑶ Correct the wind

Scrub plane opposite ends of the board to create reference points for winding sticks to help remove warp from the datum. Start in the corners and plane until you have cut the full width. Place winding sticks across the planed ends, and use them to identify where the bulk needs to be planed off.

**Technique: Correcting wind—
see p94**

Look across *the top edges to see where the wood is warped*

⑷ Smooth out the scallops

Correct the wind in the middle portion of the board. Switch to the jack plane to smooth over the scalloped surface left by the scrub, working cuts in the same direction. When trying to make a flat surface keep the sole of the plane flat on the board; when smoothing you may need to change the direction of cut depending on the grain direction. A finer plane called a smoothing plane may be used, but it is good practice to aim for a smooth surface from the jack.

CONTINUED ☞

TIP
You could use a vise or F-clamp to fix the board vertically to the work bench so that you can plane the sides horizontally.

5 Cut and plane face edge

Mark a pencil guideline for one of the long sides of the board and saw off the excess. Sawed surfaces are never straight, however, and to create a totally flat and square edge you need to true the sawed side with the jack plane. Take the opportunity to plane the sawed short edges as well. By using the plane on its side like this, you can use the flatness on the work bench and the squareness of the plane to make this cut at 90° to the face; it is always worth checking these things with a try square as well.

Raise the board on plywood to give clearance for the plane

6 Measure a parallel from the edge

You have now created a datum of one straight, flat long side from which a parallel side can be marked. A board gauge, shown here, is a useful tool for marking the new parallel edge, but definitely not necessary; a long ruler, with measurements taken from either end and joined together, will suffice. Cut off the waste with a saw or ax and plane smooth and flat. Now you have two parallel sides, the ends can be cut square. Use a try square and marking knife to mark the square ends, which can then be sawn off and planed with the low angle jack plane.

> **REMEMBER TO KEEP PLANING IN THE SAME DIRECTION, OTHERWISE THE PLANE ONLY NIBBLES AT THE PEAKS OF THE FIRST SET OF FURROWS.**

8 Plane down to the final thickness

Use the scrub then jack planes to cut a wide bevel on all sides of the board, planing down until you just reach the pencil line You can then colour in the new wide bevels with the pencil to give you a clear marker as to how far your planing has got. Keep going until you have a smooth and flat surface to the correct thickness of board.

The pencil marks *are shaved off when the surface is level all over*

7 Set the final thickness of the board

Examine the sides to identify where the wood is thinnest; this gives you the maximum thickness possible for a board with parallel flat faces. Set the marking gauge to this width and score a line all round, then highlight by running a pencil along the groove.

Press hard *on the gauge to score a line as deep as possible*

CONTINUED ☞

USING A FRAME SAW

The fewer number of teeth on a frame saw blade makes it ideal for cutting curves, as does the thinness of the blade, which facilitates turning.

To turn the blade, relieve the tension in the frame by loosening the string and then twisting the blade fixing.

To cut internal hollows, detach the blade, insert it through a drilled hole, and reattach.

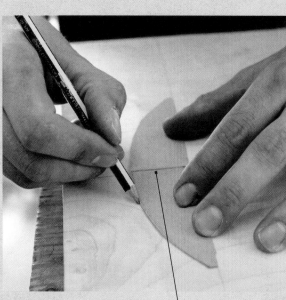

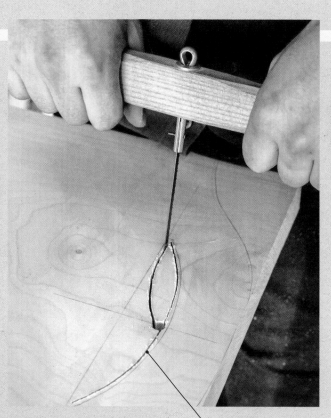

9 Mark the handle

Make a card template for the handle hole. Mark a line on the template at the midpoint, and an similar line down the midpoint of the board. Determine how wide to make the handle and draw a horizontal guideline for the base of the hole. Trace around the template, then draw the curves of the handle freehand.

A handle *width of at least 1⁹⁄₁₆in (40mm) is advisable for strength*

10 Saw the handle

Drill a ¼in (7mm) starter hole for the frame saw, close to the top of the midpoint of the handle hole, then thread through the blade; *see* Using a frame saw, above. Roughly cut out the shape of the hole, leaving a thin margin of waste next to the pencil line, then roughly saw the top curve of the handle.

Technique: Using an electric drill—see p24

Do not saw *right along or up to the guideline— leave waste for finer knife cuts*

Support your knife *hand for strength and stability*

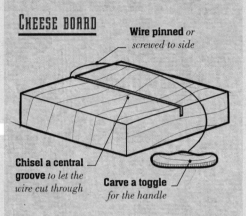

Design variations

A few simple adaptations transform the basic design into a cheese or carving board. If you cut a hole into one end of the cheese board, you could attach the wire using a second toggle.

CHEESE BOARD

Wire pinned *or screwed to side*

Chisel a central groove *to let the wire cut through*

Carve a toggle *for the handle*

CARVING BOARD

Hole *in the handle for easy storage*

Edge groove *for catching meat juices*

Cut the groove *with a gouge, drilling depth holes in the corners as guides*

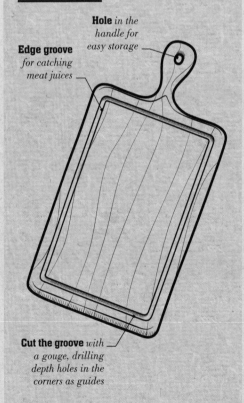

11 Refine the handle and chamfer edges

Finish cutting the handle with a straight knife, using thumb pivot grip to cut to the pencil line. Alternatively, if the board is still clamped you can use the knife in two hands working away from yourself. Resting your arms on the board and pivoting your body around the cut, you can safely refine the curve. Try to create smooth curved edges, refine the sawed surfaces, and cut a chamfer along all of the handle edges. Finally, use a jack plane to cut a chamfer along each of the straight edges of the board.

Knife grip: Thumb pivot—see p22

Technique: Carving a chamfered edge—see p16

Tilt the plane *to cut an angled chamfer*

MAKE A
Shrink Pot

The genius of this pot lies—as the name suggests—in the shrinking. The lid and base pieces are split out first, roughly shaped, and left to dry. The cylindrical main body of the pot is then shaped from green wood and fitted to the dry pieces, which allows the sides of the pot to shrink naturally to fix the base in position.

You will need

TOOLS & EQUIPMENT

- Mallets, large and small
- Froe
- Pencil, compass, and ruler
- Bench hook
- Handsaw (such as a pull saw)
- Straight knife
- Ax
- Work bench
- Auger
- Measuring gauge
- Electric drill and ⁵⁄₁₆in (8mm) drill bit
- *optional:* 180 grit abrasive paper

MATERIALS

- 1 green wood log, around 6⅞in (175mm) in both length and diameter, for the lid, knob, and base
- 1 green wood log, around 3⅛in (80mm) in both length and diameter, for the pot cylinder
- Scrap piece of wood, for the wedge

Skills

YOU WILL LEARN TO

- Form a mortise and tenon joint with wedge: *steps 11–15*

REMIND YOURSELF HOW TO

- Split with a froe: *p82*
- Use a pull saw: *p24*
- Baton with a knife: *p16*
- Correct wind: *p94*
- True with an ax: *p94*
- Use an auger: *p30*
- Use an electric drill: *p24*
- Carve a chamfered edge: *p16*

KNIFE GRIPS

- Thumb pull: *p21*
- Chest lever: *p19*
- Wrist twist: *p112*
- Pencil grip: *p28*
- Reinforced pull: *p32*
- Thumb push: *p22*
- Thumb pivot: *p22*

Design guide

The size of your shrink pot is only limited by the size of the log from which you shape the cylinder. It is sensible, however, to start with a small one, which will open the door to lots of possibilities. This size pot would be perfect for storing salt or sugar, or for keeping small trinkets in.

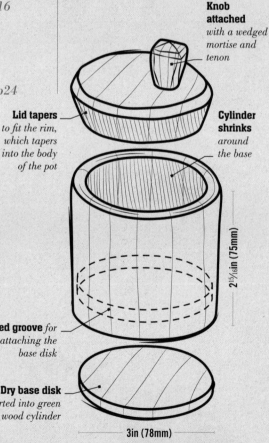

Knob attached *with a wedged mortise and tenon*

Lid tapers *to fit the rim, which tapers into the body of the pot*

Cylinder shrinks *around the base*

2¹⁵⁄₁₆in (75mm)

Angled groove *for attaching the base disk*

Dry base disk *inserted into green wood cylinder*

3in (78mm)

EXPLODED VIEW

" THIS PROJECT SHOWS
JUST HOW **LIVELY** AND
WILLING TO MOVE
WOOD CAN BE! **"**

> **USING A QUARTERSAWN PLANK** MEANS THE LID AND BASE WILL **SHRINK** WITH A **MINIMAL** AMOUNT OF **CUPPING.**

TIP
Rough shaping the lid and removing the bark helps speed up the drying process by exposing more end grain.

The Process

— **Use one half** *for the lid and knob, and split the other for the base*

1 Split out billets
With a mallet and froe, split out a plank ¾in (20mm) thick. Take it from the middle of the log where, viewed from the end, the growth rings run perpendicular to the plank. Split the plank in half down the middle, then split one of these halves lengthwise.

Technique: Splitting with a froe—see p82

2 Rough shape the lid
At one end of the thicker billet, mark a circle guideline with a radius of 3in (78mm), for the lid. Mark the straight sides of an octagon around the circle, then cut out the octagon with a saw. Tidy and rough shape with a knife, but leave the lid oversized to allow for shrinkage.

Technique: Using a pull saw—see p24

Knife grip: Thumb pull—see p21

Use a shallow, gentle action *to take thin shavings from the midpoint*

3 Shape the knob billet

Take the remaining half of the thicker billet and use a knife and mallet to baton out a rectangular bit of wood for the knob, roughly square in cross section. Use chest lever grip to shave the sides to a true square: sight the billet end for twists, then shave two adjoining surfaces flat and square, from which you can then true the other two surfaces.

Technique: Batoning with a knife—see p16

Knife grip: Chest lever—see p19

Use thumb pull grip *to clean up the sides and remove bark*

4 Flatten the base billet

Create flat parallel sides to the base billet by shaving it down slightly with an ax. Sight along the billet for any twists in the grain—known as "wind"—and even these out by taking shavings from one side. Leave these three pieces to dry for up to three weeks.

Techniques: Correcting wind, Truing with an ax—see p94

CONTINUED ☞

WRIST TWIST GRIP

Check to see if the tip of the knife blade will poke through the bottom; if it does, take extra care to avoid cutting yourself.

Wrap your fingers around the handle of the knife and make the cut by pushing the knife with the heel of your palm.

As you push the knife, twist the billet in the opposite direction; you are following the growth rings, and can therefore cut all the way around in the same direction.

5 Cut a hole for the cylinder

Take the log for the cylinder and secure it to a workbench. You could do this with wedges against uprights; or alternatively, use a vise, F-clamp, or your feet. Center the auger and bore in until a hole is cut clean through the log.

Technique: Using an auger— see p30

Wedging the log *between uprights is one way to secure it*

6 Expand the hole

Shave out the rest of the waste wood with a knife, down to a thickness of $\frac{5}{16}$in (8mm), using a wrist twist action; *see* above. Shorter shavings are easier to take, so carve out half of the pot at a time, approaching from either end in turn. Shave off the bark with chest lever grip, then use thumb pull to true the base. For larger cylinders, an incannel gouge could be used, or a series of connected smaller drill holes, or the frame saw with a good blade.

Shave the base *of the pot to a flat surface*

TIP
Make sure the base fits fairly loosely at this stage, since a tight fit could result in the wood splitting as the cylinder shrinks.

Cut the outer half first *so that you can grip the other end of the billet*

Insert the base *with the chamfered side facing out*

7 Cut the groove

Make a short pencil line inside the pot, ½in (12mm) up from the base. Set a marking gauge to this depth, tighten the screw, and score a deep line all the way around, then score a second line ⅛in (3mm) nearer the base. Chip out the wood between these lines with the point of a knife. The groove should be ³⁄₁₆in (4 or 5mm) deep; if it is too shallow, the cylinder may split upon shrinking. Cut the groove flat at the top edge and beveled at the bottom.

Knife grip: Pencil grip— see p28

Grip the blade *along the blunt top, like a pencil*

8 Shape and fit the base

Place the cylinder at one end of the base billet and draw a guideline around the inside edge. Cut out along this line for the outer half of the disk, using chest lever grip then thumb pull for finer cuts close to the line. Mark another rounded line ½in (12mm) further in, and cut a chamfer to this line. Repeat the process on the opposite side, switching to reinforced grip; leave a small section of excess wood attached to make chamfering the last section easier—then saw it off and refine with a knife. Pop in the base, making sure one side is held in the groove, then leave the pot to shrink over a couple of weeks.

Knife grip: Reinforced pull— see p32

CONTINUED ☞

SETTING THE TAPER

To determine the gradient of the taper on your lid (and rim), you can either decide to cut in by Y amount over X distance (X being the thickness of the lid); or you can pick an angle of gradient, and use a sliding bevel to mark that angle and guide your tapering cuts.

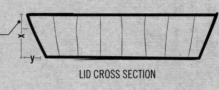

For a shallow gradient , *opt for a relatively narrow angle or width*

LID CROSS SECTION

9 Shape the lid
Place the pot top-down on the lid piece and trace around it, then shape to this guideline. Decide on the taper gradient; a shallow gradient is good for a lid. There are two ways to achieve the gradient; *see* Tapering the lid, above. We chose to taper the lid down to a specific width, marked with a circular pencil guideline.

Shape and taper *the lid using thumb pull grip*

10 Refine the rim
To fit the lid, an entirely circular edge to the rim of the pot helps immensely. Find something round to draw on a guideline, if you need it, and shave the outside edge to this line using thumb pull grip. Switch to the wrist twist to taper the inside rim to match the gradient of the lid. If you are struggling with the fit, wrap some 180 grit abrasive paper around the lid and use it to abrade the mortise to the correct shape.

Taper fairly straight *at the rim, and blend in gradually down the pot*

" FOR A TIGHT FIT, MAKE THE TENON A FRACTION WIDER THAN THE MORTISE, ESPECIALLY IF USING SOFTER WOOD. "

Take off the corners *of the sawed sides to further shape the tenon*

12 Rough shape the tenon

Saw to the required depth along the tenon length guidelines on each face. Use a knife in thumb push grip to pare away the waste material around the tenon, and the reinforced pull stroke to cut back down to the saw kerf. Cut to the square guideline, then continue to refine the shape of the tenon down to an octagon.

Knife grip: Thumb push— see p22

11 Mark the tenon

Mark a center line on each of the long faces of the knob billet, then use these lines to help you draw a square in the center of one of the ends, for the shape of the tenon. Next, mark a horizontal guideline all the way around the billet to the length of the tenon. Measure how far in from the edge of the billet the tenon will sit, and stick tape on the saw blade at this distance, to act as a guide for how deep to cut.

CONTINUED ☞

FOCUS ON...
WEDGED TENON JOINT

Fitting a wedge into a tenon helps achieve a tight fit to the joint, which is especially important if you are using softer wood. To begin with, you should aim for the tenon to be just slightly larger than the mortise. Inserting a relatively thick wedge forces apart the sides of the tenon, so that the wood fibers of the mortise and tenon compress against each other.

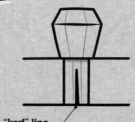

A "kerf" line
is sawed into the tenon

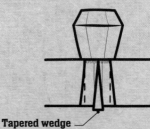

Tapered wedge
spreads the tenon for a secure fit

The shape
of the knob resembles the capital of a Doric column

Mark the width *of the mortise on the wedge billet*

13 Cut the slot and shape the knob

Saw straight down the center of the tenon to create the slot for the wedge. Shape the knob by first drawing a guideline ¼in (5mm) less than its full height, then shaving off the corners from this line down to the tenon, using thumb pivot grip. Next, shave down the flat faces, working eight sides but leaving it square at the top. Mark another guideline 5mm (¼in) beyond the first, and saw off the waste at this point.

Knife grip: Thumb pivot—see p22

14 Drill the mortise and cut a wedge

Drill a ⁵⁄₁₆in (8mm) mortise hole for the knob tenon, positioning it slightly off-center, which is most efficient for opening the lid. Baton the billet down to size with a knife and taper it to a thin ridge to form the wedge. Test fit the tenon, shaving off material if needed, then insert.

Technique: Using an electric drill—p24

Tap the wedge *with the head of an ax or small mallet*

A thick *chamfer looks attractive*

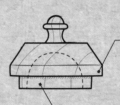

15 Tap in the wedge

Insert the tenon into the mortise. Make a mark on the wedge at two-thirds of the thickness of the lid. Tap the wedge into the tenon slot up to this mark, then use a pull saw to remove the majority of the protruding waste. For a stronger joint, glue could be used on the tenon; glue only one side of the wedge, to allow for movement of the wedge.

16 Finish shaping the lid and knob

Use a knife in thumb pull grip to clean up the remaining waste at the end of the tenon. Cut a chamfer around the top edge of the lid. Finally, shape the top of the knob by bringing the four sides to a point, and then chamfer the square edge.

Technique: Carving a chamfered edge—see p16

Design variations

Tapering the sides of the lid and pot rim is only one way to achieve a tight fit. Other options include creating a lip to the lid, or cutting slots in the side of the cylinder so that the lid sits flush.

SOLID LIPPED LID

Lid fits *with a lip, cut to match the width of the cylinder rim*

Reduce the bulk *of the solid lid by hollowing out the base*

TWO-PIECE LIPPED LID

Fitting principle *is the same as for the solid lid, but simpler to achieve*

The lip is made *by gluing together two disks of wood*

SLOTTED LID

Two opposite *wedges form a bow-tie shape*

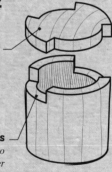

Matching slots *are cut into the cylinder*

MAKE A
FRAME SAW

The thin blade of a frame saw is good for curved cuts and reduces friction, and being interchangeable you can use the best blade for the task. Making one is a great way to practise joinery—mark out precisely and you will end up with a staple tool.

YOU WILL NEED

TOOLS & EQUIPMENT

- Jack plane
- Measuring equipment
- Pull saw
- Mallet and chisels: ⅜in (8mm) and ⅝in (16mm)
- Clamps and spare plywood
- Straight knife
- Auger
- Hacksaw or angle grinder, and safety goggles
- Metal file and metal pliers
- Electric drill, ¹⁄₁₆in (2mm) metal bit, center punch
- Lighter

- Froe, ax, and axblock
- *optional:* Plane stop, Marking knife

MATERIALS

- 3 green wood planks, split out and trued to around 1½in (37mm) wide and ⅞in (21mm) thick; *see* pp82, 94
- 1 green wood log around 1⅝in (40mm) in diameter, for the wedge
- Bandsaw blade, at least 22⁷⁄₁₆in (570mm) long
- 2 x ¹⁄₁₆in (2mm) nails
- Strong, inflexible string, e.g. starter cord for a motor, at least 3ft 11in (1.2m) long

SKILLS

YOU WILL LEARN TO

- Form a mortise-and-tenon joint—*steps 4–7*
- Use a chisel—*steps 4–7, 10–11*
- Use a marking knife—*step 5*

REMIND YOURSELF HOW TO

- Use a plane—*p100*
- Measure from a datum—*p94*
- Use a pull saw—*p24*
- Use an auger—*p30*
- Split with a froe—*p82*

KNIFE GRIPS

- Thumb pull, push—*pp21, 22*
- Reinforced pull—*p32*

DESIGN GUIDE

The frame that gives the saw its name is constructed from three pieces of wood. There should be enough space between the blade and crossbar for you to hold the saw comfortably.

Hooked tops *to arms hold the string*

Wedge used *to twist string taut*

Tightened string *places frame and blade under tension*

Mortise-and-tenon *joints hold frame together*

Recessed edges *provide handles for gripping*

18¹¹⁄₁₆in (475mm)

21¼in (540mm)

Saw blade *held in place with pins*

FRONT VIEW

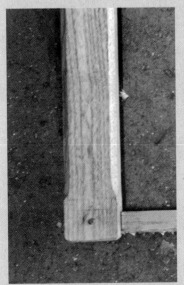 

❝ THIS FRAME SAW MAY BE **LIGHTWEIGHT,** BUT THE **WINDLASS** AND **TENSILE STRENGTH** OF THE WOOD KEEPS THE **BLADE TAUT,** WHICH MAKES **SAWING** HIGHLY **EFFICIENT. ❞**

TIP

You'll know a surface is flat if you are able to take a full length and width shaving off the surface with the plane.

The mirror surface *will show if you are sawing square*

The Process

1 Shave the planks parallel

Shave one of the wide faces of a plank to a flat datum with a jack plane. Set a measuring gauge from this datum and mark a line for the thickness, taken from the thinnest point. Emphasise the line with a sharp, hard pencil and plane down to this line to form two parallel surfaces.

Techniques: Using a plane, setting a datum—see p100

Mark the datum *face side and edge to measure from*

2 Saw the planks square

Repeat the planing process for the thinner faces, then do the same for the other planks. Now saw the planks to size, making sure you cut totally square by marking guidelines on two faces with a try square and keeping the pull saw straight. A good trick is to polish the saw surface to act as a mirror for sighting; the reflection should perfectly line up with the board.

Technique: Using a pull saw— see p24

1.

2.

1. Delicate vertical chops set the sides of the mortise and form a "shoulder" to work from. Center the chisel with your fingers before each cut, and sight against a try square to keep it vertical.

2. Tilt the chisel to lever out chips. First clear a deep V-notch in the center of the mortise, to create space to take out bigger chips and allow them to split along the grain.

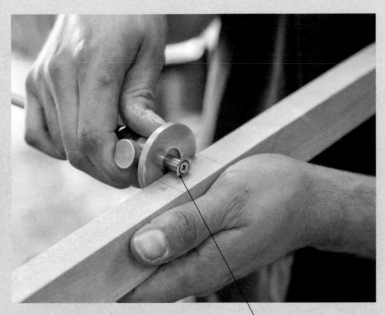

3 Draw the mortise hole

Mark out the mortise on an arm piece, starting the bottom at the halfway point and making it the same size as the tenon. Draw the top and bottom lines, then mark the mortise hole with a marking gauge. Set the width of the mortise with the mortise chisel, in this case $\frac{5}{16}$in (8mm); it should be around one-third the plank thickness. Score the side of the mortise using a marking gauge, measuring from the face. The plank is $\frac{13}{16}$in (20mm) thick, so set the gauge to $\frac{1}{4}$in (6mm).

The gauge *severs the first layer of fibers of the mortise*

4 Chisel the mortise

Chop out the mortise with a mallet and $\frac{5}{16}$in (8mm) chisel; *see* above. First make a series of shallow vertical cuts, starting from the middle and ending $\frac{1}{16}$in (2mm) shy of the end so that you can remove the wood without damaging the edge of the mortise. Make the cuts deeper until you reach a depth of 1in (25mm). Pare the waste from the ends, lining up the chisel blade exactly with the edge line. Repeat steps 3 and 4 on the second arm.

CONTINUED ☞

1. **Hold the ruler still** with one hand and press in the tip of the knife. Keep the knife still in the wood and remove the ruler.

2. **Slide the try square** along the edge until it rests against the knife. Hold the square still and score a square line.

Continue the guideline around each face by placing the knife in the corner groove left by the previous line and butting it against the try square.

1.

2.

5 Mark the tenon

Mark out a tenon at the end of the cross piece. Set the tenon length to 1in (25mm) and score a guideline on all faces with a marking knife; *see* above. To mark the tenon width, score a center line, lightly push in the chisel centered on this line, then set the gauge to the edges of the chisel mark and score round the faces.

6 Saw the tenon

Clamp the piece securely and saw two depth lines, keeping the blade straight, then saw along the grain; a tenon saw or ripsaw would work well for this. Saw diagonally along the two lines at once, tackling them from both sides, before finally sawing straight down to the shoulder.

Chisel a notch
along each scored line to help align the saw

TIP
Chamfering the end of the tenon helps it to fit in the mortise, and prevents mistakes arising from a "flaring" tenon.

Use a try square *to help you drill straight down*

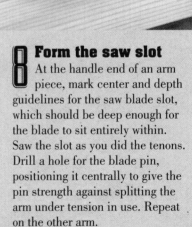

Remove **material** *where the tenon is sticking*

7 Chamfer and test the fit

Chamfer the ends of the tenon with a knife in thumb pull grip. Test the fit in the mortise: if it is too wide, pare back the cheeks with a wide chisel to keep the surface true. If both corners fit but it won't insert straight, you may need to reduce the tenon width; do this on just one side, and if needed on the other end of the crosspiece make sure you do it from the same edge.

Technique: Carving a chamfered edge—see p16

Knife grip: Thumb pull—see p21

8 Form the saw slot

At the handle end of an arm piece, mark center and depth guidelines for the saw blade slot, which should be deep enough for the blade to sit entirely within. Saw the slot as you did the tenons. Drill a hole for the blade pin, positioning it centrally to give the pin strength against splitting the arm under tension in use. Repeat on the other arm.

CONTINUED ☞

TIP
The more stop cuts, the more work with the saw— and the easier it will be to chisel out the waste.

9 Start to shape the crook

Draw the "shepherd's crook" shape at the top of an arm piece, making sure the curve is on the opposite side to the mortise so that it points outward. Drill a hole with an auger at the inside edge of the hook; a great way to get a tight curve where the string will wrap around. Mark a cross, clamp to a piece of plywood, and drill straight through.

Technique: Using an auger— see p30

10 Saw stop cuts

Remove the remaining waste with a saw and chisel. First, use a try square to draw a series of perpendicular guidelines along the slope of the crook, marking all faces and stopping just short of the sloping guideline. Saw down each of these lines, which are "stop cuts" where the chisel edge will come to rest, helping to control the chiseling action.

Don't saw beyond *the guideline— you will clean it up later*

The arms *should be mirror images in shape*

12 Refine the hook

Use the knife to continue to shape the crook. Employ thumb pull or thumb push grips to cut concave chamfers underneath, starting from a little way up the slope and pinching into the hook slightly, then to refine the top curve and chamfer the edges. Switch to reinforced grip to cut a straight, thick chamfer down the edges of the rest of the slope. Repeat steps 9–12 on the other arm.

Knife grips: Thumb push, reinforced pull—see pp22 and 32

11 Chisel the slope

Starting at the shallow end of the slope, chip out the waste with a mallet and chisel, then tidy the chiseled surface with a knife in the reinforced pull grip. Begin to shape the top of the crook by sawing off the corners.

You may need *to go over the area a few times to remove all the waste*

CONTINUED ☞

Hold the blade *over the end of a work bench*

13 Form the handle grips
Mark rectangular guidelines, on each face of the arm, for the four recesses of the handle grip, indicating the depth of the concave and where the curve will start and finish. Cut each recess, first removing a notch at either end to the depth of the concave, using the thumb push grip, then shaving down the waste between with reinforced pull. Chamfer all edges, then repeat on the other arm.

Make the recesses $5/16$–$3/8$in $(8$–$10mm)$ *deep*

14 Cut the saw blade
Put on safety goggles, and use a hacksaw or angle grinder to cut the band saw blade to the correct length. Leave the blade a little long so that the frame can bow out slightly when the blade is nailed into place, which helps create tension. Remove any sharp corners from the ends of the blade with a metal file.

TIP
Don't clamp on the teeth of the blade, as they are offset on a band saw and you risk flattening them.

> 66 POSITIONING THE SECOND PIN **SHORT** MEANS THE **FRAME** WILL BE SLIGHTLY **OFFSET**, AND HENCE REMAIN FAIRLY **SQUARE** UNDER TENSION. 99

15 Drill a pin hole
Assemble the frame, then insert the saw blade to the correct depth and flush with the arm edge. Mark the spot for the pin hole by "tickling" it with the electric drill and metal bit, then remove the blade from the arm. Clamp the blade on scrap wood, hammer a center punch on the mark, and, wearing safety goggles, drill the hole.

16 Drill second hole and pin saw
Measure between the centers of the pin holes on the frame, and subtract ⅛in (3mm) to give you the position of the second drill point. Mark with a pen, then center punch and drill, as before. Test fit the nails for pinning the blades, clip them to size with metal pliers, and file off any sharp edges. Pin the blade in place.

Clip the waste
so that the nail is flush with the frame

CONTINUED ☞

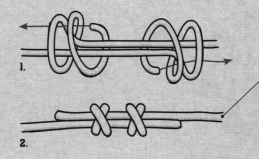

DOUBLE FISHERMAN'S KNOT

1. Place the two ends of the string side by side. Loosely wind both ends twice around the other to form two loops. If you wound the first end over the other string, wind the second end under the first.

2. Pull the ends back through the two loops to tighten, then pull them again to bring the two parts of the knot together.

Pull the longer ends *of the string to slide the knots together*

1.

2.

17 Attach the string

Wrap the string around the hooks of the arms and cut to length, leaving $3^{15}/_{16}$in (100mm) of slack for tying the knot. Tie the ends together with a double fisherman's knot; *see above*. Fuse the ends by melting them with a lighter so that they don't fray and unravel.

The loop *should be slack enough to take off, but still under tension*

18 Form the wedge

Split out a billet for the wedge, around $1^{7}/_{16}$in (35mm) wide and $^{5}/_{8}$in (16mm) thick, taking it from a tangent rather than radius of the log, for strength. Chop off the bark with an ax and shape it into a wedge with a slight taper at one end. Use a knife and reinforced pull to remove any sharp edges, then chamfer the top and bottom with thumb pull grip.

Technique: Splitting with a froe—see p82

Design variations

We have opted for a simple slot and pin method of attaching the blade. Here are a couple of options for alternatives that, while much more complicated, allow the blade to be rotated.

SPLIT PIN

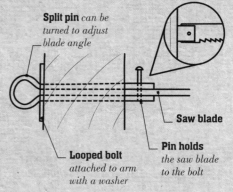

Split pin *can be turned to adjust blade angle*

Saw blade

Looped bolt *attached to arm with a washer*

Pin holds *the saw blade to the bolt*

WOODEN HANDLES

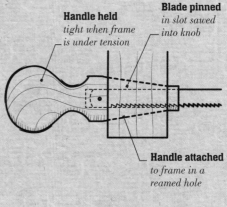

Handle held *tight when frame is under tension*

Blade pinned *in slot sawed into knob*

Handle attached *to frame in a reamed hole*

19 Attach the wedge

To place the saw under tension, start to twist the string with your fingers until a slot appears in the middle. Insert the wedge in the slot and use it to continue to twist the string, until the saw is under a lot of tension: ping the blade and you should be able to hear when it has changed key. Leave the saw untensioned when not in use, otherwise you will stretch the blade.

> ❝ LEAVE THE SAW UNTENSIONED WHEN NOT IN USE TO AVOID STRETCHING THE BLADE. ❞

MAKE A
FRAME STOOL

This project explores the tensile properties of wood, and provides an introduction to post and rung joinery, a simple and adaptable style of furniture making. The seat is woven from the diskarded rubber inner tubes of bicycles, a resource that may otherwise go to landfill, and results in a very comfortable sitting experience.

YOU WILL NEED

TOOLS & EQUIPMENT
- Measuring equipment
- Knife and small log or mallet
- Marking gauge
- Large and small froes, large mallet
- Shaving horse and draw knife
- ½in (12mm) tapered tenon cutter
- Set square
- Workbench
- Bench hook
- Pull saw
- 2 large F-clamps
- Spare thin pieces of wood
- Hammer and nail
- Electric drill with ¼in (6mm) and ³⁄₁₆in (5mm) bits
- ½in (12mm) reamer
- Marker
- Paintbrush
- Wood glue
- *optional*: Compass or dividers, cleaving brake

MATERIALS
- 1 or more green wood logs, around 23⅝in (600mm) long
- Smaller, dry piece of the same wood, at least 2 x ¾ x ³⁄₈in (50 x 18 x 9mm), for the pegs
- Plank of "2 x 4"
- Old bicycle inner tubes (often available free from bike shops); cleaned, valves cut off, and rough patches sanded smooth

SKILLS

YOU WILL LEARN TO
- Use a tenon cutter: *step 11*
- Make a jig: *step 13*
- Ream holes with a drill: *step 15*
- Peg joints: *steps 18–19*

REMIND YOURSELF HOW TO
- Baton with a knife: *p16*
- Split with a froe: *p82*
- Use a draw knife: *p94*
- Correct wind: *p94*
- Form a tapered tenon: *p56*
- Use a pull saw: *p24*
- Use an electric drill: *p24*
- Level legs: *p154*

KNIFE GRIPS
- Thumb pull: *p21*
- Thumb pivot: *p22*

DESIGN GUIDE

The stool follows a basic frame design using long and short rungs set at different heights. The joints need to be very strong to resist the high degree of torque (twisting force) created by the woven inner tubes. Tapered tenons are a lot stronger than straight tenons, and are given additional strength by being glued and pegged. Note that the rung measurements shown include the lengths of the tenons.

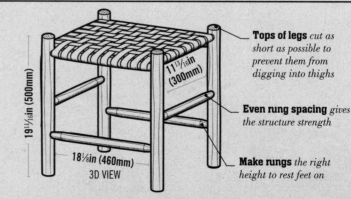

19¹¹⁄₁₆in (500mm)

11¹³⁄₁₆in (300mm)

18⅛in (460mm)
3D VIEW

Tops of legs *cut as short as possible to prevent them from digging into thighs*

Even rung spacing *gives the structure strength*

Make rungs *the right height to rest feet on*

" TAPERED JOINTS ARE STRONG AND ELEGANT.
IT IS IMPORTANT THAT THE TENONS LINE UP ON EITHER END
OF EACH RUNG TO AVOID GAPS AROUND THE MORTISES,
SO MEASURE ACCURATELY. "

> **66** THE **THINNER** THE **WIDTH** OF A SECTION OF WOOD COMPARED TO ITS **LENGTH**, THE EASIER IT IS TO **CONTROL** THE **SPLIT**. **99**

The Process

1 Make 16 pegs

Saw a small, dry billet to about 2in (50mm) long. Split this billet into ⅜ x ⅜in (9 x 9mm) sections, then split one of those in half and half again to create four pegs each about ³⁄₁₆in (4.5mm) wide. A marking gauge is helpful for measuring out these pegs. You will need a total of 16. Chamfer both ends of each peg using thumb pivot grip.

Technique: Batoning with a knife—see p18

Knife grips: Thumb pull, thumb pivot—see pp21, 22

2 Mark and split the log

Split out billets for four legs, 1⁹⁄₁₆in (40mm) in diameter, and two long rungs and four short rungs, each 1in (26mm) in diameter. Plan a cleaving strategy to make the most efficient use of the wood. Mark the components to see how they might split out; a compass or dividers can be useful. Using a large mallet and froe, split the log in half and half again, then into two quarter wedges, along the line. If you need to split the wood into thirds, do this early, leaving the majority of cleaving as simple halving.

Push with your knee *and lever the sides apart with the froe*

Technique: Splitting with a froe—see p82

Cleaving brakes hold the end of a piece of wood as you split it, and help to control the split. By levering against the cleaving brake you are able to pry apart the wood and apply strain to the chosen side of the split.

Place the wood into the middle of the brake with the bottom end pointing away from you. The side of the billet that you want the split to run toward should always be facing down; when you push down on the froe, you will create tension where it is needed.

3 Split out legs and rungs
For the finer divisions, use a smaller mallet and froe and, if you have one, a cleaving brake; *see* above. Put tension on the thicker side (if there is one) by pushing down on the froe blade, then levering the split open with your elbow against the handle of the froe, pulling it toward you. Without a cleaving brake, the wood can be cleaved against the ground with the thin side down. If the split starts running off, flip the billet around and put pressure on the other side to control it.

Ignore the circles *at this point and split the wood down the middle, as accurately as you can*

4 Start shaping a leg
Take a leg billet and use a draw knife on a shaving horse to create a straight datum, from which the other sides can be measured. Set the datum on the bark side, since the outside of a tree tends to have more tension than the inside, and the wood is likely to be more bowed. Start by taking short shavings off the ends of the billet, then work your way in toward the center—at the very center you may only need to skim off the bark. Flip it around to work the other half.

Techniques: Using a draw knife, correcting wind—see p94

CONTINUED ☞

> " THE GROWTH RINGS ON A BILLET SUCH AS THIS CAN ACT LIKE CONTOUR LINES ON A MAP—REMOVE THE HILLS TO CREATE A FLAT SURFACE WITH PARALLEL LINES. "

Shave down in three facets, *taking off the corners, rather than trying to take single wide shavings*

5 Square a leg billet

With a pencil, mark a 1³/₄in (45mm) square at one end of the leg billet, measuring from the datum. Your piece of wood may well be wedge-shaped rather than cuboid, so adjust your cuts accordingly. Make sure this side is straight all the way down; you can rest the billet against the side of the shaving horse to gauge where material needs to be removed. Repeat on the remaining two sides, so that the cross section of your leg is square.

6 Make the square leg octagonal

Clamp the leg at 45° and shave off the corner to create a new flat facet. Work around the whole leg, shaving off each corner so the square ends become octagonal. Widen the corner facets and shave off more material, until all eight faces are parallel and the same width.

TIP
Mark each component with letters or numbers to keep track of which tenon goes in which mortise.

Keep the shavings *thin and in long curls*

7 Shave to a cylinder

Now turn the octagonal leg into a cylinder by taking off each corner. You do not need to shave off much wood here; thin shavings off each corner will create a rounded shape. Continue working on the leg until it is smooth. Repeat steps 3–6 to make three more identical legs, then make eight rungs the same way; each should be about 1in (25mm) in diameter.

8 Mark tenons on the rungs

Draw a cross on the end of a rung, as close to the center as possible; this will help you cut the tenon straight. Measure 3⅛in (80mm) down from the end and draw a ring around the rung. The tenon will taper to an 5⁄16in (8mm) point along this length. However, the wood will shrink before you assemble the chair, so at this stage you should make the end of the tenon slightly larger, at ½in (12mm) wide. Draw a ½in- (12mm) diameter circle over the center of the cross, for guidance.

CONTINUED ☞

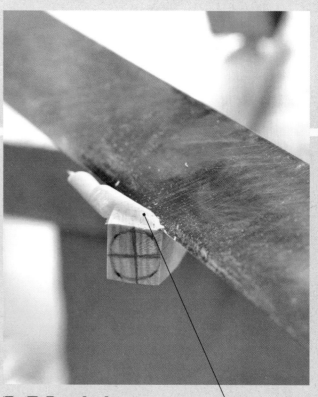

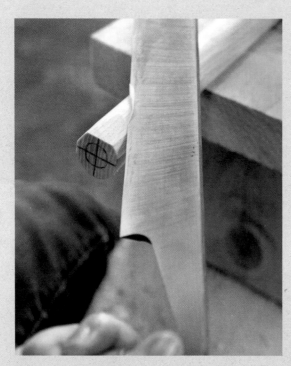

9 Start tapering the tenon

To shape the tenon, start the taper with a draw knife, taking off short shavings on one side of the rung. Begin at the tip of the tenon, where you need to take off more material, then work your way back to the line little by little.

Technique: Forming a tapered tenon—see p56

10 Rough shape the tenon end

Use the same square–octagon–circle technique shown in steps 5–7 to shape the end of the tenon, creating an even square first before taking off the corners to form a cone. Use the pencil circle as a guide, but leave a little waste to be finished with the tenon cutter.

Be careful *not to make the surface of the tenon concave*

"TAPERED TENONS ARE FAIRLY FORGIVING: IF YOU SHAVE OFF TOO MUCH, THE TENON WILL SIMPLY TRAVEL FURTHER INTO THE MORTISE, AND WEDGE JUST AS TIGHTLY."

11 Shape further with a tenon cutter

Place a ½in (12mm) tenon cutter onto the end of your tenon, aligning it centrally; the gap between the wood and cutter should be even all the way around. Hold the cutter in your nondominant hand and twist the rung clockwise to shave off material, exactly like using a pencil sharpener. At this point, only use the tenon cutter on the first half of the tenon, to allow for shrinkage. Repeat steps 8–11 on both ends of all eight rungs.

Center the tenon *then focus on the widest part*

12 Finish the tenons once dry

Leave the rungs to dry for 2–3 weeks, then work on them again with the tenon cutter, shaving material off until each tenon reaches the pencil line. You may need to use a draw knife to skim off any slight shoulders around the last third of each tenon first. The end points of these tenons should now measure 5/16in (8mm) in diameter. It is important that the rungs are the correct length, and that the tenons taper by the same amount; if one rung is too short, you will either have to remake it, or shorten all the other rungs to match it.

CONTINUED ☞

MAKING A JIG

A jig is the name given to a custom made tool designed to hold items in place, so that they can be worked on safely and efficiently. The round legs of the stool are liable to roll around on the workbench, and are difficult to clamp. This jig provides a rest for the legs to sit in, and makes it possible to clamp them securely and work on them together.

Offcut placed *over the legs to give a surface for clamping*

9/16in (15mm)   9/16in (15mm)   9/16in (15mm)

1in (25mm)

1¹⁵/₁₆in (50mm)   1¹⁵/₁₆in (50mm)

Recesses *sized to make a secure but comfortable fit*

13 Make jigs to hold the legs

You will need to make two jigs in order to clamp the legs. Measure 5¹¹/₁₆in (145mm) from the end of a "2 x 4" plank and mark it with a pencil line. Then, using a set square for accuracy, mark the measurements shown in the diagram above. Secure the plank on your workbench with a bench hook, and use a saw to cut out triangular areas for the stool legs to lie in. Saw off the jig at the 5¹¹/₁₆in (145mm) line.

Technique: Using a pull saw— see p24

14 Drill holes in the legs

Place two legs in the jigs, on your workbench. Make two pencil crosses on each leg, at 1⁹/₁₆in (40mm) and 10¼in (260mm) from the top, sighting down the legs and using a ruler to make sure they are exactly central. Clamp the legs to the bench using an F-clamp and a small scrap piece of wood. Drill holes at the crosses with a ²/₈in (6mm) drill bit, sighting with a try square to keep them straight.

Technique: Using an electric drill—see p24

Lightly tap on *a nail to make a center punch for the drill bit*

CONTINUED ☛

It is much easier *to shorten the tenons than to extend the mortises*

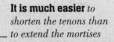

15 Ream the holes

Now taper the mortises to match the tenons; it is important to get the right depth for the holes at this point. The maximum width of the hole should be ¹¹⁄₁₆in (17mm), so find the point where the reaming attachment is at this width and mark it with a pen: you need to ream to this depth. Now ream down until the mark is aligned with the highest point of the edge of the hole. Reamers have very sharp cutting edges: make sure the pieces are secure, and keep the blades far away from your fingers!

Ream straight down *until the pen mark is level with the top of the wood*

16 Check the measurements

Once you have reamed all eight holes, dry fit the side panels and check that they match. Make sure the tenons are fully fitted to the reamed mortises, and check that the legs are parallel. If they are not, you need to shorten one or more of the rungs. Measure the length of each rung from the outside edges of the legs: they should all be the same length. If you have rungs of different lengths, find the shortest one and use the tenon cutter to adjust the other rungs to match it, checking them continually as you go.

CLAMPING THE PANELS

Two large F-clamps are needed to keep the side panel secure and held together tightly until the joints are pegged.

One clamp squeezes the legs and rungs together, while the other attaches the panel to the bench and holds it true and flat.

A scrap piece of wood placed over the middle of the rungs enables the panel to be held evenly in place by the second clamp.

17 Glue the tenons

Apply a small amount of wood glue to the inside of each mortise in one of the two side panels, swirling the brush around to coat evenly. Attach the rungs, then clamp the side tightly to hold everything in place while you insert the pegs; *see* above.

18 Drill holes for the pegs

Mark a cross on each leg, centered on the tenon and one-third of the tenon depth in from the inside edge of the leg. Center punch the mark with a nail and hammer, then drill straight down all the way through the leg, using a ³⁄₁₆in (5mm) drill bit. Start by drilling at an angle, toward the center of the leg, to avoid the drill bit scooting off the curve; then quickly shift to drilling straight down, avoiding bending the drill bit.

TIP

Once the mortises are glued, work quickly to clamp the panels in the right position, then take your time with the pegs.

> HAVING THE FRONT AND REAR RUNGS LOWER CREATES A SLIGHT CURVE IN THE SEAT, MAKING IT MORE COMFORTABLE.

19 Hammer in the pegs

Lubricate each peg with some glue on the end third, before hammering it in square to the stool; the tapered ends of the pegs should come out the other side. Use a knife in thumb pull grip to remove the ends of the pegs where they stick out. Repeat steps 17–19 on the other panel.

Knife grip: Thumb pull— see p21

Shave down *the protruding peg ends flush to the leg*

20 Assemble the front and back

Choose which side of each frame will face out based on what looks best to you; for instance, if the legs bend, you may want to avoid having them turn inward. Mark holes for the upper rungs by measuring $^{13}/_{16}$in (20mm) down from the center of the first upper tenon and marking a cross; for the lower rungs, measure $3\frac{1}{2}$in (90mm) down from the first lower tenon. Then repeat steps 14–20 to insert the remaining rungs into the legs.

Measure carefully *to ensure consistent spacing*

CONTINUED ☞

21 Weave the warp

Clamp the stool frame and tie the first tube to the corner of an upper side rung with a simple double knot. Bring the tube down and under the opposite rung, then up around and back to the starting point. Cover up the knot, and continue winding around in this way until you reach the opposite corner; the warp should be fairly tight.

Join one tube *to the next on the underside of the seat, with a sheet bend knot*

22 Weave the weft

To cross over from warp to weft, thread the inner tube under the adjacent rung at the corner, then bring it around and start weaving in and out of the warp, following the repeating pattern, above right. You can make the weft very tight, to give strength to the seat. When you reach the diagonally opposite corner, fold the end of the last inner tube underneath the seat. Weave the tube in and out of the warp under the seat to provide friction, then tie it off with a double knot halfway down the underside of the weft.

Form the pattern by weaving with the weft tubes, here shown horizontally.

Line 1—Lift over two and thread under two, repeating to the end.

Line 2—Lift over one tube, then proceed as for line 1, threading under and over two tubes.

Line 3—Start by threading under two tubes.

Line 4—Start by threading under one tube.

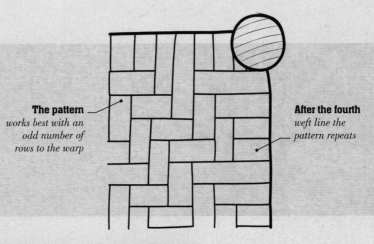

The pattern *works best with an odd number of rows to the warp*

After the fourth *weft line the pattern repeats*

Remove any protruding *tenon ends using thumb pivot grip*

23 Even out the legs

To finish off the stool, saw off about 1in (25mm) from the top of each of the legs. Then use a knife in thumb pull grip to shave the top of the sawn surfaces and chamfer the edges, creating a neat finish. Check that the stool is level, and remove wood from the bottoms of the legs as necessary, making them all the same length.

Technique: Leveling legs—see p154

Design variations

The seat can be woven from other materials, such as elm bast or hickory bark for an organic feel. If you are using bark for the seat, weaker straight tenons could be used to join the components. By playing around with the proportions of the frame, you can construct a table, or add height and multiple rungs to make a shelving unit.

TABLE

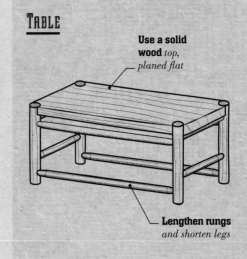

Use a solid wood *top, planed flat*

Lengthen rungs *and shorten legs*

CHAPTER 03
TURNING

Introduce turning wood on a pole lathe to your growing repertoire of skills, as your woodcraft journey culminates in the sculpting and construction of a beautiful chair.

MAKE A
POTATO MASHER

This simple kitchen utensil works much better than the more usual perforated type of masher, and making it is a great way to hone your turning skills. Once you have mastered planing cuts and rolling a bead, you will be ready to turn the spindles, posts, and legs of the Captain's Chair project that follows.

YOU WILL NEED

TOOLS & EQUIPMENT
- Pole lathe (*see pp224–45*)
- ⅛in (4mm) gimlet
- Oil
- Roughing out gouge
- Square chisel
- Spindle gouge
- Skew chisel
- Pencil and ruler

- Pull saw
- Spoon knife
- Straight knife

MATERIALS
- Cylindrical billet of green wood, about 12¹³⁄₁₆in (325mm) in length and 3⅛in (80mm) in diameter

SKILLS

YOU WILL LEARN TO
- Fit a billet to a lathe: *steps 1–2*
- Turn to size: *steps 3–4*
- Square ends: *step 5*
- Shape on the lathe: *steps 6, 10*
- Turn a bead, ball, and cove: *steps 7–9*

REMIND YOURSELF HOW TO
- Use a pull saw: *p24*

KNIFE GRIPS
- Thumb pull: *p21*

DESIGN GUIDE

Girth is retained at the masher end to give weight and surface area for the mashing action, and the tapered body gives greater access to corners of pans. The ball and bead offer gripping points, as well as decoration.

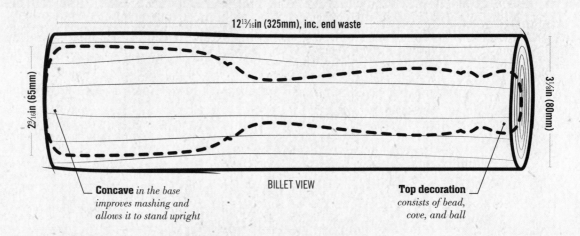

12¹³⁄₁₆in (325mm), inc. end waste

2⁹⁄₁₆in (65mm)

3⅛in (80mm)

BILLET VIEW

Concave *in the base improves mashing and allows it to stand upright*

Top decoration *consists of bead, cove, and ball*

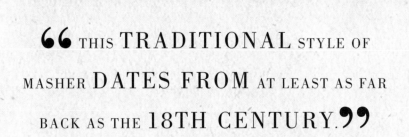

❝ THIS **TRADITIONAL** STYLE OF MASHER **DATES FROM** AT LEAST AS FAR BACK AS THE **18TH CENTURY. ❞**

66 LIFT THE CHISEL OFF THE WOOD WHEN YOU LIFT YOUR FOOT OFF THE TREADLE. 99

TIP
Punching the centers with a gimlet helps the billet spin freely on the lathe without flying off.

The Process

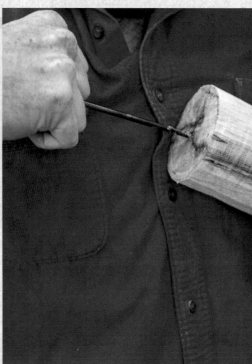

1 Center the billet
Start by placing your billet on the turning centers of the pole lathe. Judge by eye where to position them, and aim to find the midpoint of the whole cylinder overall, not just the ends. Squeeze the ends just enough to hold it in place, then spin it all the way around to see if the position needs adjusting in any direction. If the cylinder is centred correctly it should run parallel with the tool rest. If one side is off then it can be gently tapped at the end to center.

2 Punch and oil end holes
Crank the handle to push in the centers, then take the billet off the lathe. Use a ⅛in (4mm) gimlet to deepen the marks made by the centers. Twist the gimlet into the wood until you can no longer see the lead screw, then pull out. Insert a drop of oil in each hole to reduce friction. Then place the billet behind the string, wrap the string around it twice, and position the billet securely on the centers. If the string is wrapped around correctly the billet will spin down towards the tool rest.

MAKING PLANING CUTS

1. Without spinning, take a thin shaving with the tool on the rest to get an idea how to angle it; remember to have the bevel rubbing.

2. Avoid catching the trailing tip: a risk if you angle the chisel too low, as shown.

3. Use the tip to guide you: it is easiest to use the first third of the edge closest to the leading tip. Skimming a fine shaving with the very tip engaged gives great accuracy.

Wrap the string
around the opposite end of the billet from where you are cutting

3 Rough out the shape

Hold the roughing out gouge so the bevel rubs against the wood and raise the handle to engage the cutting edge. Move the gouge along, taking off shavings to create an even surface – go halfway across, then flip it round to do the other side. Look at the profile of the billet, rather than at the tool; take the peaks off then smooth into the round. When trying to get the bevel to rub on the raised, rather than lower, parts of the billet, do not push the bevel in as it will just move inwards to the lower parts. Instead, proceed the tool a small amount and hold it there as the wood spins; run a couple of passes like this before smoothing it in, edging bit by bit, roughing out a section at a time.

4 Create a smooth cylinder

. Switch to a square chisel taking off wider shavings for a smooth surface. Angle the blade to make cuts, skimming along with the tip of the chisel; try not to let the trailing end catch (see above). For a really straight cylinder, for a rolling pin, for example, you can rub a wax crayon on a straight edged bit of wood and hold it on to the billet as you turn.

CONTINUED ☞

SQUARE AND V-NOTCH CUTS

The method is essentially the same for cutting the square end of a piece and the V-notch of a bead. Both are made by rubbing only the edge of the bevel against the wood, and all cutting is done with the tip of the blade edge. To square the end, hold the corner of the bevel head-on; for a V-notch, tilt the chisel so that the bevel is at the desired angle.

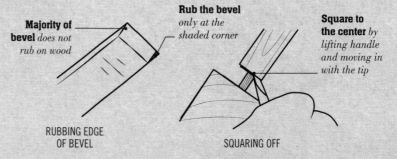

Majority of bevel *does not rub on wood*

Rub the bevel *only at the shaded corner*

Square to the center *by lifting handle and moving in with the tip*

RUBBING EDGE OF BEVEL

SQUARING OFF

Leave about ¾in (20mm) of wood around the center

5 Square the ends

To square an end with the spindle gouge, first create a little shoulder, going in straight with the flute vertical and the bevel rubbing underneath. Then turn the gouge on its side to cut across the end toward the center, resting the bevel on the shoulder. Take care not to damage the gouge by hitting the centers. For a flatter, smoother finish, switch to a skew chisel to finish off the end.

6 Remove waste from the handle end

Move the string to what will be the masher end. The handle should constitute about two-thirds of the total length of the masher. Begin building up a concave cut to form the neck. In the center of the valley you are creating, hold the tool straight, and on the sides, angle the tool toward the center. When you are happy with the thickness at the masher end, remove material from the rest of the handle, keeping the top section relatively flat.

SHAPING A BALL AND BEAD

Lift the handle and roll the chisel, pivoting your hand on the tool rest. The more skewed the cut, the sooner you come out of the lift-and-roll and the smoother the curve. Once the skew edge is vertical any more rolling may cause the corner to catch. Instead, bring the handle around by pivoting the bevel on the bead, and slide the body of the chisel along the tool rest.

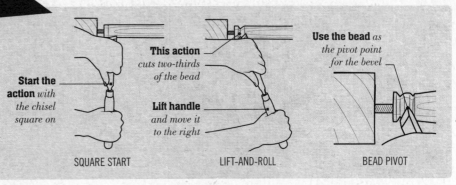

Start the action *with the chisel square on*

SQUARE START

This action *cuts two-thirds of the bead*

Lift handle *and move it to the right*

LIFT-AND-ROLL

Use the bead *as the pivot point for the bevel*

BEAD PIVOT

7 Begin the decoration

Move the string to around the neck of the masher and shift your attention to decorating the top end. Decide on the widths of the ball, cove, and bead, then measure and draw pencil guidelines on the billet, allowing for waste next to the centers. Score straight in over the pencil lines with the tip of the skew, maintaining an even pressure. Start off lightly, and once you are happy with the placement of each groove, push further in.

Spin faster *for a smoother finish on the decoration*

8 Round the ball and bead

Begin shaping the ball at the top of the handle by making a V-notch with the toe of the skew. Do not to let the edge of the skew catch. Work alternately on either end of the ball to create the steepest parts of the curve—the most difficult sections of the ball. Then work your way from the middle, using the heel in a rolling cut, to create a smooth sphere. Use the same technique to make the tighter radius for the bead; *see above.*

CONTINUED ☞

TIP
As you work you will find the centers wear in, so tighten the billet accordingly from time to time. If they squeak, add more oil.

Make the widest *part of the handle about one-third of the way down*

Hold the skew *sideways to shape between curves*

9 Make the cove
Continue working with the skew to make a triangular peak between the two grooves that border the cove section; this leaves neat shoulders either side of the cove and is far easier to do prior to gouge work. Switch to the spindle gouge to take off the peak of the triangle and cut a cove. Be careful not to remove too much here; if you do go too far with the spindle gouge, it is difficult to re-shape on either side with the skew.

Aim for a *shallow but defined depression*

10 Clean up the handle
Move the string back to the end of the masher while you refine the handle; having the string placed at the widest part of the masher means it will turn slower, and greater rotation speed helps effect smoother cuts, so treadle extra fast to make up for it. Use the skew for fussy sections, and the square chisel for gentle slopes, to blend the shape of the handle into an even curve. First cut a convex, working to the edge of the bead on one side, then work down the gradual slope of the handle, blending it into the concave section. Keep your top hand loose enough to let the chisel slide, and delicately push the bevel onto the wood.

> *UNLIKE A GOUGE, A* **SKEW CHISEL** *WILL* **OFTEN** *NEED TO BE* **SHARPENED** *AS YOU WORK.*

Design variations

Make a juicer or pestle for a mortar by carving a bulbous end on a smaller billet. The juicer grooves are started by drawing evenly spaced radius lines at the bulbous end, from which the straight lines can be marked with dividers.

JUICER

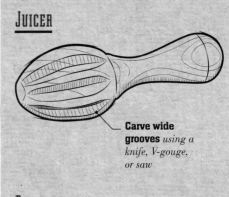

Carve wide grooves *using a knife, V-gouge, or saw*

PESTLE

The handle *should fit snugly in a clenched fist*

Make the crushing *end wide and flat*

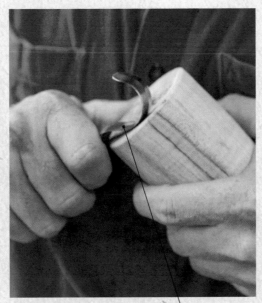

Draw the knife *toward you, rotating the masher*

11 Add a V-cut

These are added for aesthetic interest at the point where a convex blends into a concave; they draw the eye in and distract from any imperfections in the transition. Go in straight with the toe, then square up and neaten the edge created with the heal, coming back from the handle end. Then put the string back into the neck and, with the square chisel, smooth the convex into the notch.

12 Trim the ends

Remove a little more of the waste beyond the ball. Take the masher out, and saw off the protruding ends with a pull saw. Use a spoon knife in thumb pull grip to carve off the last of the waste at the masher end; because we turned this end slightly concave, a straight knife would leave a little knobby bit. Trim the waste at the ball end with a straight knife, also in thumb pull grip.

MAKE A
CAPTAIN'S CHAIR

Crafting a chair draws upon all the skills and techniques learned by working through all the projects in this book. If you are confident in your abilities, this beautiful chair should mark the satisfying culmination of your mini apprenticeship. The design is based on a traditional captain's style, but without the need for steam bending of the arms and crest.

YOU WILL NEED

TOOLS & EQUIPMENT

- Pencil and measuring equipment, including metal ruler and pair of compasses
- Ax and axblock
- Drawknife and shaving horse; see p214
- Electric drill with drill bits and reamer attachment
- Straight knife
- Pole lathe; see p224
- Roughing gouge
- Square and skew turning chisels
- Vernier or caliper gauge
- Tenon cutter
- Mortise block
- Auger
- Tape (for marking depth on auger and drill bits)
- Scorp
- Bowl gouge(s)
- Frame saw
- Bench hook
- Swizzle sticks
- Clamps

MATERIALS

- Tracing paper and pricking pin for templates
- PVA glue
- For the crest: 1 straight-sided billet of green wood, a little larger than the sizes indicated on the templates; this could also be sawn from dry wood
- For the turned elements: 14 x green wood cleft billets; split the legs and stretchers first as any fails in these will probably work out for posts
- For the seat: section of plank 2in (51mm) thick, planed flat and parallel; see p100
- For the arms: 2 x straight-sided billets of green or dry wood, a little larger than the sizes indicated on the template
- For wedges and pegs: billets of wood in contrasting hues
- Offcuts for block and wedges to size the legs

SKILLS

YOU WILL LEARN TO

- Use tracing paper templates: *steps 1, 17*
- Make and use a mortise block: *step 16*
- Use a scorp: *step 24*

REMIND YOURSELF HOW TO

- Shape with an ax: *p50*
- Use a drawknife: *p94*
- Use an electric drill: *p24*
- Cut a chamfered finish: *p16*
- Fit a billet to a lathe: *p146*
- Turn to size on a lathe: *p146*
- Use a tenon cutter: *p130*
- Turn a bead on a lathe: *p146*
- Drill angled holes: *p56*
- Use a reamer: *p130*
- Use a bowl gouge: *p82*
- Form a mortise and tenon joint with wedge: *p108*
- Peg joints: *p130*

> 66 MAKE SURE YOU HAVE **HONED** YOUR **TURNING** **SKILLS** BEFORE EMBARKING ON THIS PROJECT. 99

DESIGN GUIDE

Use these diagrams to guide you as you shape the components of your chair. All the turned pieces—the legs, the spindles, the arm posts, and the stretchers—are made whilst the wood is still green, and then left to dry, and shrink, before being finished. This shrinkage should always be taken into account when measuring; follow the dimensions in the diagrams below.

The scale templates for the arms, seat, crest base, and crest can be photocopied at 326 per cent. The dotted lines on the seat template diagram represent sightlines—you should sight down these lines when drilling the holes for the armposts and spindles. The angles indicated on the seat template are the angles at which the mortises should be drilled.

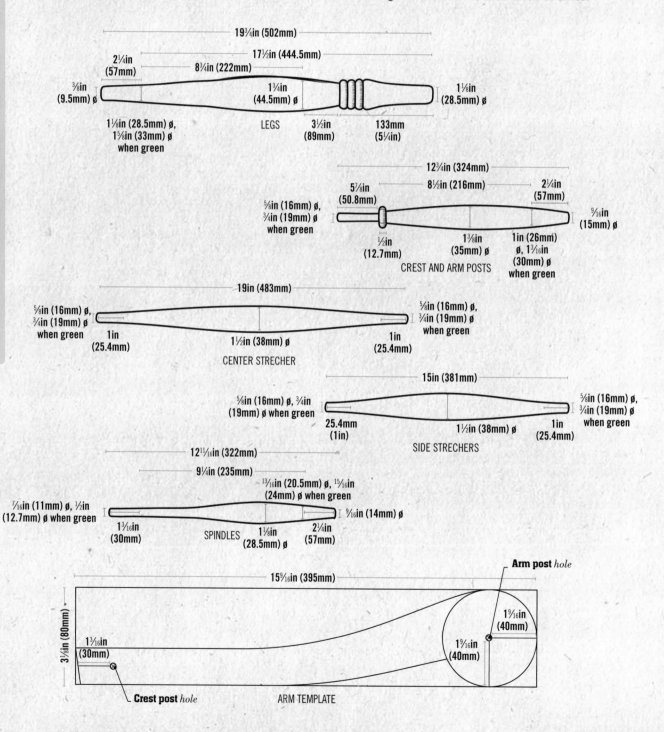

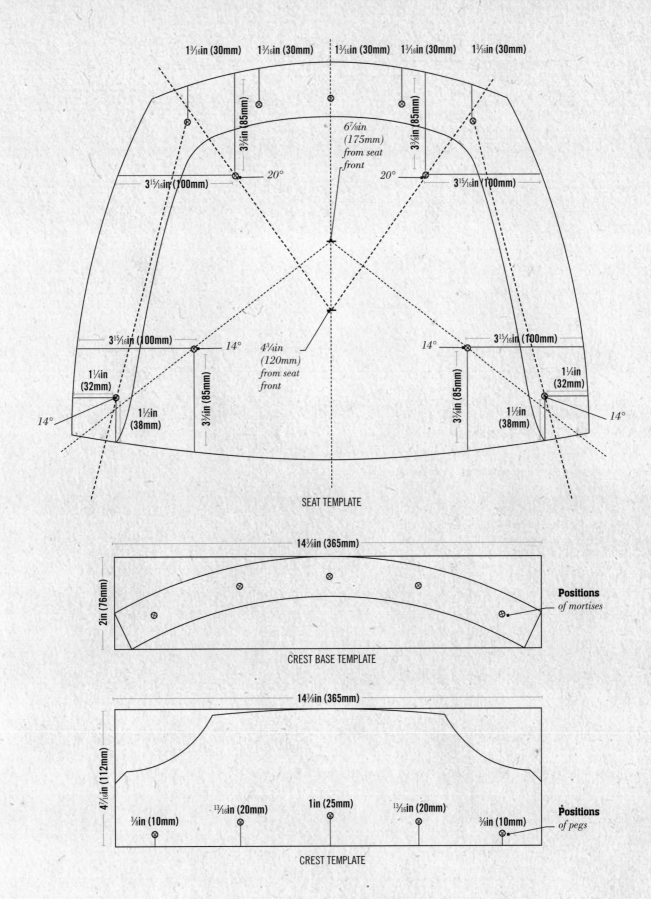

1³⁄₁₆in (30mm)   1³⁄₁₆in (30mm)   1³⁄₁₆in (30mm)   1³⁄₁₆in (30mm)   1³⁄₁₆in (30mm)

3³⁄₈in (85mm)

3³⁄₈in (85mm)

6⁷⁄₈in
(175mm)
from seat
front

20°   20°

3¹⁵⁄₁₆in (100mm)   3¹⁵⁄₁₆in (100mm)

3¹⁵⁄₁₆in (100mm)   3¹⁵⁄₁₆in (100mm)

14°   14°

4³⁄₄in
(120mm)
from seat
front

1¼in
(32mm)

3³⁄₈in (85mm)   3³⁄₈in (85mm)

1¼in
(32mm)

14°   1½in   1½in   14°
         (38mm)   (38mm)

SEAT TEMPLATE

14³⁄₈in (365mm)

2in (76mm)

Positions
of mortises

CREST BASE TEMPLATE

14³⁄₈in (365mm)

4⁷⁄₁₆in (112mm)

³⁄₈in (10mm)   1³⁄₁₆in (20mm)   1in (25mm)   1³⁄₁₆in (20mm)   ³⁄₈in (10mm)

Positions
of pegs

CREST TEMPLATE

TIP

If it's hard to work the center of the crest with a drawknife, try carving across the grain with a gouge to avoid tearing in.

The Process

1 Mark the crest outline

Use the template to transfer the curved shape of the crest and center points of the spindle and post mortise holes to the base of the crest billet. Mark by pricking holes through tracing paper into the wood and joining the dots to form a pencil guideline. Mark the outline on the top of the billet, too, but not the mortise holes.

2 Shape the curving body

Rough shape to the guidelines with an ax, starting in the middle and working back out to the edge. When forming the curves, remember the grain direction changes at the deepest point of the curve and needs to be worked to or from the center. For safety when axing the parts closest to the ends, lay the crest on the block and use the edge of the block as a stop: aim the ax to carve and then follow through into the edge of the block.

Technique: Shaping with an ax—see p50

Give plenty of clearance *so there is no risk of the lead screw protruding*

Shape a gentle curve *to the top of the lumbar area, between the scallops*

3 Drill mortises and set the side scallops

Refine the basic shaping with a drawknife on a shaving horse. While the crest is still easy to clamp, drill holes 1³⁄₁₆in (30mm) deep at the mortise points on the base, marking with tape the depth on the drill bit. (When the crest has dried, you may need to redrill with the same bit if they have closed up a little in shrinking.) Now hold the bit against the front of the crest and aligned with a post mortise. Mark a line to indicate the depth of the mortise and another line higher up, well clear of the bit. Repeat at the other end, then draw out the scalloped sides of the crest so that they come in just above the clearance lines.

Technique: Using a drawknife, using an electric drill—see pp94 and 24

4 Finish shaping the crest

Chop out the scalloped sides with an ax. To give lumbar support, the front of the crest rises up straight initially, before tilting backwards by 9–10° from where the side curves begin. Work this profile into the main body of the crest, then go over the crest again with a drawknife to finesse shaping and smooth the surface. Refine further and chamfer all edges with a straight knife. Leave the crest to dry for about seven weeks; the first week should be gentle, then it could be placed somewhere warm to speed things up.

Technique: Carving a chamfered edge—see p16

CONTINUED ☞

> **TENON CUTTERS** MAKE LIFE **EASY**. WITH **PRACTICE** YOU CAN **LEARN** TO TAPER **ENTIRELY** ON THE **LATHE**.

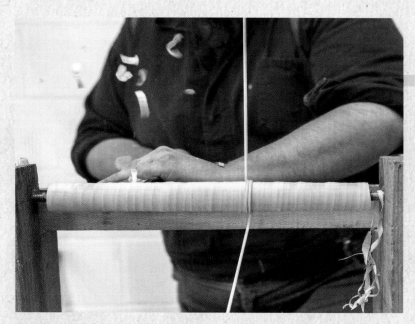

5 Size a spindle cylinder

Center and fit a spindle billet to the lathe. Start turning with a roughing gouge, taking it down in size and shaping it to a cylinder of the maximum diameter. To judge the size, taper one end thinner than the maximum diameter, then set a vernier or caliper gauge to the maximum diameter and slide it along from the thin end until it catches. Mark that point with a pencil line and turn the rest of the cylinder until it is level with this guide, switching to a large square chisel to take off wider shavings for a smooth finish. Before you begin turning the tenons, note that you turn them wider when green to allow for shrinkage and that the initial taper is short. Tenons are re-turned when dry with a longer taper but at the same gradient. It is critical that the full length of the taper is flat and at the correct length and angle.

Techniques: Fitting a billet to a lathe, turning to size—see p146

6 Turn the seat tenon

The tenons are turned longer than needed to 2¼in (57mm), for some leeway. Ensure you are accurate with the size of the taper and with the location of the widest point of the tenon on the spindle. Turn solely on the lathe, or use a tenon cutter as well. Taper to the tenon on the lathe, blending the convex of the spindle bulge into the tenon, which needs to have a flat surface. Remove enough material to fit the tenon cutter.

Technique: Turning a taper— see p146

TIP
Green wood turned so thin can fly off. Use sharp tools and set the string close to the metal center on the fatter side, to avoid.

A "shoulder" *left by the cutter indicates the extra material to remove on the lathe*

7 Switch to a tenon cutter

Remove the spindle from the lathe and give it a few twists in the tenon cutter, making sure to keep the spindle centered in the cutter. The benefit of using the cutter is to help set a correct angle to the taper. Remount the spindle on the lathe and finish turning the tenon, copying with your chisel the angle set by the cutter. Use a caliper set to the right diameter and be certain you maintain the maximum diameter at the correct location on the spindle.

Technique: Using a tenon cutter— see p130

8 Turn the crest tenon

Turn to size the other half of the spindle. The tenon into the crest is straight rather than tapering. The width is set halfway along the spindle, tapering down from the fattest point to give a long straight run in to the crest mortise. Leave the end ⅜in (10mm) oversized so that the centre marks from the lathe can be sawn off. Turning green wood so thin can be tricky (*see* Tip, above) and you may find it easier when dry; if so, leave the crest tenon end thick and finish turning once the spindle has dried.

CONTINUED ☞

> **REMEMBER** THAT MOST **TENONS** NEED TO BE LEFT **WIDER** AND WITH A **SHORTER** **TAPER** TO ACCOUNT FOR **SHRINKAGE.**

9 Finish the non-beaded components and start on a leg

Follow the same process in steps 5 to 8 to turn the other spindles and the symmetrically tapered stretchers. Now select a leg billet and turn it to a cylinder of the correct maximum diameter. Mark a pencil line at 3¾in (95mm) for the start of the bead decoration and then ½in (12mm) apart for each of the four V-notches for the beads.

Technique: Turning a bead—see p146

10 Set up the beads and taper the end

Score straight grooves at the pencil lines for the bead with the tip of a skew chisel. Switching to the square chisel, taper the end to a shallow concave with the correct diameter and final finish. This part can now be used for the string and since it is a thinner diameter the wood will spin faster and give better results for the beads. Set up the beads by cutting four V-notches at the grooves.

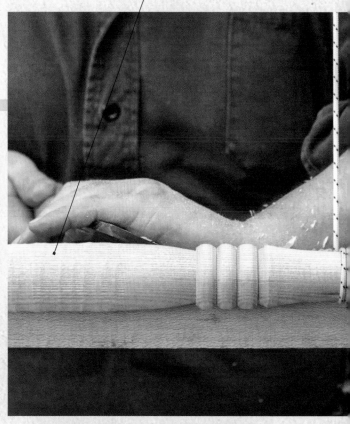

TIP

For good control, keep
the tool rest close to the
turning piece and lift off the
chisel when you take your
foot off the treadle.

Keep the maxium
diameter 1¾in (44.5mm)

11 Shape the leg beads

Shape the curved sides of the
beads. Take your time to get
your body position correct and think
where you need to end up at the end of
each cut. It is usually helpful to round
the same side of each of the three beads
before switching your body around and
doing the other side of the same three.
Score a line at the point of greatest
diameter, which is where the stretcher
tenon will be fitted.

Rest the bevel
*against the wood
surface to help
angle the cut*

12 Turn the rest of the leg

Curve a taper from the scoreline, but
without touching it, back towards the
beads. Be very careful for the last ¹⁄₁₆in (2mm)
before reaching the top bead so as to not damage
it. At the other end, take the last third of the leg
down close to the maximum green diameter of
the tenon. Gently curve a convex taper from the
scoreline, again without touching it, towards
the tenon end, to blend with the previous cuts.
Mark the widest point of the tenon measured
from the score line and taper to the correct
dimensions. Repeat steps 10 to 12 to turn the
other three legs.

CONTINUED ☞

TIP
Keep the turned pieces somewhere warm and dry, such as an airing cupboard, so that they shrink fully before being fitted.

13 Size and mark up an arm post

With a roughing gouge and then square chisel, turn an arm post billet to a perfect cylinder 1⅜in (35mm) in diameter. Measure and mark the tapered tenon, then measure up from the top of the tapered tenon to mark the top of the bead. Mark another line ½in (12.7mm) back for the base of the bead.

14 Turn the arm post bead

Switching to the skew chisel, use the tip to cut straight grooves at the bead lines. Set up the beads by cutting V-notches at the grooves. Round the sides of bead as described in step 11.

Turn the tenon *until no high points are indicated*

15 Finish shaping the arm post

Taper the main body of the post down to the base of the bead. Beyond the top of the bead, turn the cylinder down to a diameter of ¾in (19mm) to form a straight tenon for the arm mortise, allowing for shrinkage. Repeat steps 13 to 15 to form the second arm post and the two crest posts. Leave all the turned pieces to dry for one to two weeks. Check the diameter of pieces regularly to verify when they have finished drying, allowing for 10 per cent tangential shrinkage. Alternatively, weigh the components regularly and once their weight is steady for a few days, you will know they are dry.

16 Turn the dried pieces

After drying, check the diameters of each tenon and re-turn them to the correct size. Mortise blocks are a good way to fine tune tenons. Make them by reaming the correct mortise in an offcut, then saw the block accurately in half. Cover the inside of the mortise with pencil lead, then give it a few turns around the tenon. Any high points will be revealed by pencil marks, which you can use as a guide for where to remove more material. Once the tenon matches the block you will get a solid block of graphite on the tenon.

Techniques: Squaring the ends, reaming holes with a drill—see pp146 and 130

CONTINUED ☞

TIP

An auger drill bit with an extender is helpful, as the extra length amplifies your ability to sight angles accurately.

17 Mark the seat

Transfer the seat template to tracing paper and mark on to the pre-planed plank the outline of the seat and guidelines for the post and spindle decks. Mark crosses to indicate the position of each mortise hole, and also draw on any sightlines; it is along these lines that you set the angle for drilling and reaming angled mortises. The sightlines for the legs will need to be re-drawn on to the underside for reaming; they are drilled from the top, reamed from the bottom.

18 Drill leg holes

Drill a leg mortise hole to the correct width and angle. Set the angle with a sliding bevel and try square, measuring from 90° upright. Through its height, the try square shows the plane of the sightline; align the bevel within this plane and lean the drill back accordingly. Mark with tape the drilling depth, which matches the tenon length. Ideally, get someone to help sight the angle as you drill. Drill all seat holes in the same way, following any angles and sightlines.

Technique: Drilling angled holes—see p56

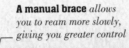
A manual brace *allows you to ream more slowly, giving you greater control*

Line up the extender *with the scoreline of the other leg*

19 Ream leg holes

Fit a reamer for the leg holes to a brace or electric drill. Mark the reaming depth on the side of the bit with pen. Ream the hole to the same angle it was drilled at, and sight as for drilling. Test the fit by first measuring the distance from the seat to the scoreline, aiming for 8¾in (222mm). This is where the stretchers will be fitted and also acts as a fixed point for verifying the fit. Insert the leg and measure from the scored lined with a divider; if it falls short, measure how much and ream to this depth. Test several times and get it right.

Technique: Use a reamer—see p130

20 Drill stretcher holes

Ream and dry fit the other legs. As you fit each leg, mark a number or letter on the corresponding leg and hole to avoid any mix-ups at the final fit. Mark points for drilling the mortise holes on the scored stretcher lines of one pair of front and back legs. The growth rings in the stretchers should be 90° degrees to the grain direction in the component with the mortise, so the tenons don't split the mortises with changes in humidity. Wrap tape on the drill bit to the correct mortise depth. Since you cannot drill straight across, to avoid drilling at an angle and missing the diameter line, twist the leg so that it is around 2mm (¹⁄₁₆in) offset, or whatever makes the mortise centred on the stretcher. Position the bit on the mortise mark and carefully line it up level with both stretcher score lines, then drill. Turn around and repeat on the opposite leg, then drill stretcher mortises on the other pair of legs.

CONTINUED ☛

TIP
Measure the mortise
depth and distance
between the legs from the
same point, to take account
of the curved surface of
the stretcher.

Measure from *the outermost edge of the mortise rims*

21 Check lengths and re-turn

Work out the final lengths of the stretchers by measuring the distance between the mortise holes, then adding on the mortise depths. Transfer to the stretchers, always measuring from the center points. Re-turn the stretchers to size, making square cuts with the skew on the stretcher side, and angled-in V-cuts on the waste side; a small chamfer on the tenon can also help when fitting. Saw off the waste end and tidy with a knife.

22 Drill holes for the middle stretcher

Dry fit the side stretchers, twisting them so that their growth rings are 90° to those of the legs; this is the grain orientation so that the most movement caused by humidity changes will occur along the length of the leg and not across it, which risks splitting. Mark a centrally positioned drill hole at the midpoint of the bulge on each stretcher. Wrap tape on the bit to the mortise depth. Again, since you cannot drill straight across, to avoid drilling at an angle, twist the stretcher so that it is ¹⁄₁₆in (2mm) offset, before lining up the drill bit between the stretchers. Drill and repeat on the opposite side.

Grip the scorp with your arms tucked in so that the scraping action comes from your whole body.

Keep the action fast and follow the sequence of: start cut, follow through, then lift, unless you can see clearance behind.

Take care! As soon as you see the wood fibers starting to tear, change the direction of your cuts.

23 Mark the seat hollow

Freehand draw the shape of the hollow onto one side of the seat, including the buttock indent and the line of the "pommel," which is the central raised section toward the front of the seat that demarcates the thigh indents. Leave at least ⅜in (6mm) clearance from the spindle deck. To ensure symmetry, copy the lines onto tracing paper, then flip the paper and transfer to the other side. Drill two ¾in (18.5mm) depth holes to indicate how deep to carve the hollow, drilling either side of the center line toward the rear of the buttock indent.

24 Excavate the hollow

Start carving out the buttock indent, using a bowl gouge and mallet to cut across the grain, always towards and only as far as the center line; this step could also be done with an adze. Taper the indent up towards the pommel line, excavating until the depth holes no longer appear. Switch to a scorp—a tool with a wider radius than the gouge that leaves a fine finish—to smooth over the gouged surface of the indent and blend it in with the edge of the spindle deck and up to the pommel; *see* above. If you don't have a scorp, use a shallower bowl gouge instead, taking off fine shavings.

Technique: Using a bowl gouge—see p82

CONTINUED ☞

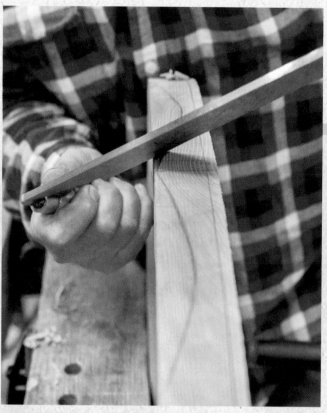

TIP
You can cut the chamfer by eye, or mark equidistant guidelines on the seat and side faces to ensure consistent width.

25 Excavate the thigh scallops

Cut out the front edge of the seat with a frame saw, then draw guidelines for the thigh scallops, which should come down to between a half and two-thirds of the depth of the seat, leaving the pommel in between them. Mark the center of the seat and the edge of each arm deck, then mark the lowest point of each scallop midway between and freehand draw curved lines connecting the points. Hollow the scallops with a drawknife, skewing it to cut across the grain. Cut a steep bevel initially, to the full depth of the scallop at the front, then roll it back into the seat by taking off corners in a series of progressively wider and shallower cuts.

26 Finish the seat

Blend in the thigh scallops with the buttock indent, first with the drawknife and then scorp or bowl gouge for finer blending. Saw out the back and sides of the seat, then return to the drawknife to cut a thick chamfer along all the sharp edges, and refine the sawed surface across all faces.

Hold the drawknife *on the skew as you cut across grain*

Keep checking *that you are following the guideline*

Use a mallet *to firmly fit the legs into their mortises*

Mark orientation *lines from legs to stretchers and between stretchers*

27 Saw slots in the legs and dry fit the undercarriage

Dry fit the legs and mark center lines across the end; they should be at 90° to the grain direction in the seat (left to right) so that when the wedges are inserted they don't split the grain. Mark center lines down the sides of each tenon to help saw straight. Saw slots down these lines to, at most, three-quarters of the tenon length; the joint wedges are inserted into these slots. Dry fit the legs with the stretchers to form the undercarriage. Mark leg numbers or letters on the side stretchers, and draw orientation lines running from the central stretcher to side stretchers, so that you can realign when gluing.

28 Glue and fit the undercarriage

Take the undercarriage apart and then glue it together in stages, starting with the two side panels and then joining them together with the central stretcher. Apply the glue to the surface of each mortise hole with a swizzle stick, working quickly before the glue sets, and match up numbers and orientation lines. When the stretchers are all glued, bang home the leg tenons: the sound of the whack goes up an octave when they are fully inserted.

CONTINUED ☞

MAKING WEDGES AND PEGS

Once the wood has been battened to small blocks, pegs and wedges can be made easily with a large, flat chisel.

1 For wedges: Support the block on a bench hook upright. With both hands on the chisel, use your body weight to pare the block to a taper. The wedge should be a fraction wider than the end of tenon, with parallel sides to the thin end.

2 For the pegs: Using a ¾in (5mm) drill bit for sizing, pare down the wood to square sides, then remove the corners with a knife to form an octagon. Chamfer both ends to prevent the fibers from fluffing.

Wedges need to be just a little bit wider than the tenon

29 Wedge the leg tenons

Make four wedges for the leg joints; *see* above. Glue and knock the wedges into the sawed tenon slots. Apply glue to only one side of the wedges, as otherwise they can come loose when the slots expand due to atmospheric changes: glued on one side they will stay stuck to that side of the slot until it closes back up again. Tap in the wedge with the back of an ax, hammer, or small mallet.

Technique: Wedging a tenon and mortise joint—see p108

30 Remove the wedge waste

Once the glue has dried, saw off most of the protruding waste and pare the rest with a bowl gouge. Be sure to protect the seat surface when sawing. One option is to clamp a flexible metal ruler to the seat and against the wedge, and to use the ruler as a protective surface to saw against. When paring with the gouge you are cutting across end grain, so only cut to the middle and move around the tenon; once down level with the seat you can take a single cut right across.

Technique: Pegging joints—see p130

31 Drill spindle peg holes
Now attach and peg the spindles. Mark center lines from the spindle mortises down the back edge of the seat. Apply glue to a mortise and tap the spindle into place. At the midpoint of the center line, drill a ³⁄₁₆in (5mm) hole, 1¾in (45mm) deep, straight down through the seat and the center of the spindle. Repeat for the other spindles.

Hold the spindle *and rest your arm on the seat to keep everything steady*

32 Insert the pegs and true
Put a dab of glue on a peg and tap it into the hole with the back of an ax, hammer, or small mallet. Tap until you hear the pitch change, which means it has hit the back of the hole. Saw off most of the waste and pare away the remnants with a chisel or drawknife. Repeat for the other spindles.

CONTINUED ☞

TIP

Mark the mortise positions with crosses and place the center point of the drill bit precisely on the crossing point.

Drill all the way *through the billet*

33 Draw an arm

Mark the shape of the arm on a billet. At one end of the billet, and offset to one side, draw a circle with a radius 1⁹⁄₁₆in (40mm) for the hand rest. At the opposite end and on the opposite side, mark a width of 1⁹⁄₁₆in (40mm) and draw a straight line to one-third of the length of the billet. Join this straight line and parallel straight edge to the circumference of the circle with pleasing curves, making space for a person's body to sit comfortably and keeping the grain aligned for strength at the crest end. Dry fit the arm posts and measure between the center of their tenons to work out the mortise hole positions. Mark these points, then drill a straight hole to the diameter of the arm post tenon through the centre of the hand rest.

34 Start shaping the arm

Shape the arm with an ax and refine with a drawknife. Since the arm posts lean at 14° but the crest posts are perpendicular to the deck, the base of the arm must be shaped on the diagonal to fit square to the crest post. Test fit the arm; you may need to take a shaving or two from under the arm post mortise to allow the arm to sit back on to the crest post. Mark a line level with the top of the bead, and shave the base side to this angle. Shave the top of the arm parallel to this new datum, and taper it to the correct dimensions so that the back is slightly thinner than the front, which enables the arm to pleasingly tilt back, and is thin enough so that the crest can fit on to all of the post and spindle tenons.

36 Finish shaping the arm

Finish shaping the arm by rounding the hand end and creating a nice curved facet. Accentuate the curves back towards the crest; this allows the hand end to be rounded all the way back into this facet, which then continues back down the arm. The arm will stick out behind the crest; it can be sawed reasonably flush, but you may prefer the rustic look of it sticking out and there should be some length behind the hole for strength. If making from green wood, leave the arms to dry for eight weeks, drying gently for the first week.

35 Drill the crest post mortise

Place the arm on its arm post and hold the back flat against the bead of the crest post. Measure across from the tenon and mark on centrally the position of the crest post hole. Drill the hole square.

CONTINUED ☞

> **MAKING PEGS FROM WOOD OF CONTRASTING COLOR TURNS A PRACTICAL ELEMENT INTO A DECORATIVE FEATURE.**

37 Attach the arms

Saw notches for wedges into both tenons of the arm posts, but just the seat tenons of the crest posts. Apply glue to the arm post mortise holes and to the seat mortise of the crest post, then fit the posts, attach the arm, and knock in the posts with a mallet. Glue and tap a wedge into the handle tenon of each arm post. Saw off most of the underseat excess of the arm and crest post tenons, leaving them slightly proud. Glue and tap in the wedges, then remove the excess.

38 Fit the crest

Make sure the spindle tenons are roughly equal in length to go into the crest, and that they are not so long that they bottom out in the mortises. Fit the crest piece on to the spindles and posts, and peg the tenons as per steps 31 and 32. Position the pegs for the crest posts at ⅜in (10mm) up from the base of the crest, ¹³⁄₁₆in (20mm) up for the two outer spindles, and 1in (25mm) up for the central spindle, to achieve a pleasing curve to the peg positions that echoes the overall curve of the crest.

Cut a pencil in half
*so that it lies flush to
the top of the block*

39 Measure the leg heights

The final job is to level the legs. Sit the chair on a completely flat surface. Place a ruler horizontally near the front of the seat and measure the height of each front leg with another ruler; if there is a discrepancy the legs will need to be shortened. For comfort, the chair has a ½in (12mm) tilt from the pommel to the spindle deck, achieved by cutting the back legs shorter than the front. Measure the height at the back of the chair to determine how much you need to lower the back legs.

40 Wedge the legs level and cut to size

Insert small pieces of wood, or coins, under the legs until they are all level. Measure the distance from the floor to the bottom of the shortest leg, and cut a wood block to this height. Use the block to draw guidelines around the three longer legs, bearing in mind the back legs need to sit shorter for the tilt. Saw off the excess and cut a chamfer around the base of each leg with a knife in thumb pull grip.

CHAPTER 04

TOOLS

Get a handle on the key tools you need to craft with confidence. Discover their features, uses, and safety points, as well as how to sharpen and care for them so that they perform well and last.

USING
TOOLS FOR SHARPENING

Sharpening tends to be done with abrasives, particles of a hard material that are used to scratch away the metal of the tool. This is usually done in a way that creates or maintains a specific shape, with progressively finer abrasives being used in succession to polish the edge. A polished edge not only cuts better, but also stays sharper longer. Abrasives come in many forms, including sheets, bench stones, and diamond-plated metal plates.

The Process

GRINDER

■ **For general re-sharpening** a watercooled bench grinder is preferable. The slower speed of this machine makes it easy to control, and the grindstone is cooled by water, which prevents overheating and removes debris.

■ **The hollow ground** profile created by a bench grinder is very beneficial for many sharpening tasks, particularly for tools that need short flat bevels, such as axes and knives.

FILES

■ **Files can also be useful** for rough shaping of axes if you don't have the luxury of a motorized grinder, and they are necessary for sharpening saws.

■ **Most modern saws** are not designed to be sharpened, but learning to sharpen a saw is nevertheless a useful skill.

■ **Files can also be used** to sharpen large augers—do not sharpen the outside of augers, though, as this changes the size of the hole they cut.

Use two files, *one triangular and one round; always use a round file on a concave surface*

TYPES OF BEVELS

1. Flat bevel The bevels on cutting tools often need to be ground and honed flat, in order to smoothly guide the edge into the cut.

2. Hollow bevel A hollow ground surface allows you to create a flat bevel more easily and quickly, and is very good at returning a convex bevel to flat. Hollow grinding should be the preferred way for axes and knives.

3. Micro bevel A micro bevel—which is another, much smaller bevel at a steeper angle from the main bevel—is very useful for removing burrs and preventing edge roll. Unlike that of a secondary bevel, the edge on a micro bevel is still able to sever the fibers before they are split by the primary bevels.

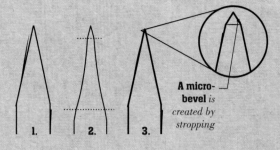

1. **2.** **3.**

A micro-bevel *is created by stropping*

ABRASIVE PAPER

■ **Use a dowel** wrapped with wet and dry abrasive paper to sharpen the blade of a spoon knife, and other curved blades.

■ **It can help to rest** the knife on a raised block—if you just rest it on the table, you may find it gets in the way of the dowel.

■ **Try to find the flat surface** by feel, making sure to work away from the edge and all the way around, and reposition the blade so that it is supported where needed.

■ **Abrasive paper** can also be used for flattening, using float glass as the flat substrate to put the paper on.

Use a diamond lapping plate *to flatten a waterstone: draw a wavy pencil line on the surface of the stone, then rub the lapping plate against it until the marks disappear*

JAPANESE WATERSTONE

■ **Japanese waterstones** are very efficient at cutting. They come in a variety of rough or fine grades; the number given refers to the number of particles, 600 grit being much rougher than 2500 grit.

■ **What makes them special** is how soft they are, continually revealing fresh sharp particles as the stone wears down. These are hard ceramic particles with sharp corners; as the stone is used, the particles lose their effectiveness, but if the block wears down to reveal new untouched particles it will sharpen tools efficiently again.

■ **Rough stones remove** more metal, but even fine stones remove quite a lot, meaning you can work quickly.

■ **The pictured stone** should be lubricated with water as it is used, and some will need soaking beforehand.

CONTINUED

TIP
Long whetstones make it easier to move the tool in a flat motion—this is harder to gauge with a small slipstone.

> **REMOVE MATERIAL IN LAYERS PARALLEL TO THE BEVEL, MAINTAINING THE ANGLE AT THE POINT OF THE BLADE.**

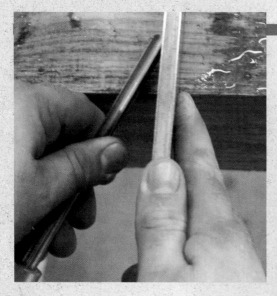

Metal particles *taken off the tool will clog up the stone—clean them off with a simple pencil eraser*

Bench stones

■ **Bench stones are so called** because they are usually large and used while supported on a bench; they tend to be solid ceramic blocks. The pictured technique works particularly well with a diamond stone as they are light and easy to hold. Because everything is held steady on the bench and you are looking down on to the bevel, it is easy to line up and accurately position your abrasions.

■ **Rest both the gouge** and the stone on the bench and, sighting down the bevel, use your left hand to guide and push the bevel against the stone, while moving the stone back and forth with your right hand in a flat motion.

■ **High-quality diamond stones** remain flat and last for a long time. This is very useful for when the bevel of a tool needs to be flat or accurate, but the blade itself is an ungainly shape or size, such that moving the tool across a fixed stone leads to inaccuracies.

Honing guide

■ **You can use a honing guide** when sharpening chisels and planes on a bench stone. This allows you more control, which is particularly useful when you need an accurate secondary bevel, or just a very accurate flat bevel.

■ **Honing guides also work** very well with abrasive sheets that have been glued onto large flat surfaces—float glass is sometimes used, since it is particularly flat.

FEELING FOR A BURR

Once enough material has been removed, the abrasive will push a tiny "burr" over the edge blade that can be felt hanging over the other side of the blade. Feel for it gently with the tip of your finger, brushing off the bevel away from the blade edge so as not to cut yourself. While the burr will tell you that you have sharpened right to the edge, it does not necessarily mean you have created a flat bevel.

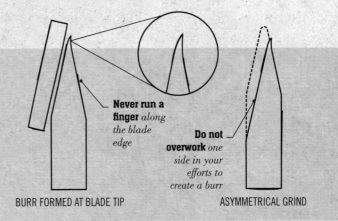

Never run a finger *along the blade edge*

Do not overwork *one side in your efforts to create a burr*

BURR FORMED AT BLADE TIP   ASYMMETRICAL GRIND

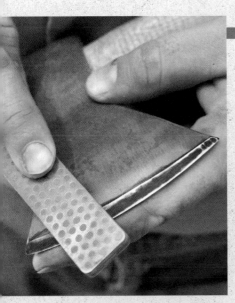

SMALL DIAMOND STONE

■ **To flatten off the hollow grind** on an ax head, use a felt tip marker to draw on the bevel, then hone with a small diamond stone. As the blade is flattened, parallel silver lines appear through the pen marks.

■ **Do this on the bench** to protect your fingers: place the ax with the blade set just in from edge of the bench, so your knuckles are against the side of the bench as you sharpen safely away from the cutting edge.

■ **Using the marker pen** is a useful technique because it lets you see what is happening. If the bevel is convex, for instance, a silver line will appear quickly in the middle of the inky bevel; to flatten a convex you work to expand the silver outward until all of the pen is removed from the bevel.

SLIPSTONE

■ **Slipstones are small abrasive stones** with a curved edge used for sharpening the flutes of gouges. Unlike bench stones, they are held in the hand during use.

■ **They can also be used** on straight knives to sharpen a flat surface. Place your finger on the other side of the stone, above where the bevel is, to hold the stone flat on the bevel; this works well with a small diamond stone too.

STROP

■ **Stropping is the final finishing step** in sharpening. Stropping can and should be used on most tools for the final polish and as a technique to brighten an edge between sharpenings. Stropping tools, or strops, tend to be made of wood or leather; if you can't plane a board very flat then a man-made board can be used effectively.

■ **Apply honing compound** to the strop and let it dry a little; Tormek paste is a good option as it is non-waxy and can be cleaned easily. Drag the edge of the blade up and down the strop. Move it away from the edge, which would dig into the blade. You are aiming to push the bevel onto the wood firmly enough to hold it flat. Keep working both sides of the edge until it gets polished and any burr is removed, being careful not to round the edge.

■ **Leather strops** can lead to rounding the edge over, which is problematic for many tools that should have flat bevels.

UNDERSTANDING A
STRAIGHT KNIFE

Mastering a basic wood carving knife is the foundation of green woodworking. This Scandinavian-style Mora knife, with its laminated blade and utilitarian handle, is the steadfast companion of any woodcrafter.

Laminated steel
makes the blade durable

Symmetrical
handle means it can be used in all knife grips

Rivet or peen
holds the tang at the base

Metal ferrule
keeps together the wood fibres of the handle

FOCUS ON...
ATTACHING THE HANDLE

As an individual at home, drilling stepped holes to house the varying shape of the knife tang can be difficult; a technique that works well is "burning in." Drill a small hole through the handle and heat up the tang, but do not heat the edge. With the blade clamped in position, tap the handle onto the hot tang, opening up the hole where necessary.

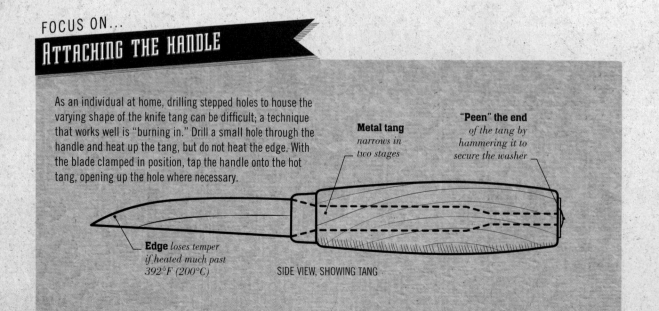

Metal tang
narrows in two stages

"Peen" the end
of the tang by hammering it to secure the washer

Edge *loses temper if heated much past 392°F (200°C)*

SIDE VIEW, SHOWING TANG

> ❝ THE "SCANDI" GRIND IS SYNONYMOUS WITH THE ART OF WHITTLING. ❞

Tapering blade
varies the length of the bevel

FEATURES

■ **Laminated blade** The blade has hard steel in the center to maintain the cutting edge longer. Softer steel on the outside gives strength and makes it easier to sharpen.

■ **Fixed blade** Many hand knives feature folding blades, but a fixed blade is much more preferable, as it gives the knife more reliable cutting action.

■ **No finger guard** The lack of a finger guard makes it easier to form grips and get in close to the blade in order to direct the cutting edge with your fingers.

USES

■ **Carving and finishing** Use for whittling and as a tool for finishing edges and surfaces of larger projects.

■ **Splitting** Can be used to split out billets from small logs and start splits before inserting wooden wedges.

■ **Chip carving** Chip out details for decoration with the tip, including letter and figure carving, or carve out small square holes.

Safety Tips

— **Keep the knife** in its sheath when not in use and never walk with the blade exposed.

— **Take regular breaks** to maintain concentration.

— **Practice knife grips** thoroughly without cutting at first. Make sure you know the "stops" that prevent the knife from carrying through, and how to keep safe should the tool slip, by ensuring no fingers are in the path of the cutting action.

HOW TO
SHARPEN

The bevel needs to be very flat on a straight knife. Resist the temptation to sharpen the edge only, which alters the blade geometry.

The Geometry

The bevel needs to be long enough to guide the edge on a flat planing cut, but short enough to make tight concave cuts. A long bevel will dig into a tight curve and have a weak edge.

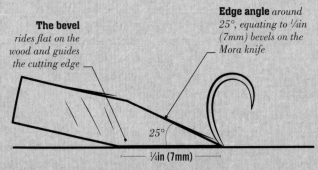

The bevel *rides flat on the wood and guides the cutting edge*

Edge angle *around 25°, equating to ¼in (7mm) bevels on the Mora knife*

25°

¼in (7mm)

Cross section of blade

The Process

1 Flatten the bevels
Make sure the abrasive you are using is flat, and move the abrasive in a flat motion in relation to the knife, or vice versa. Remove equal amounts of material parallel to the bevel on either side. Lift the handle very slightly to maintain contact at the tip.

2 Hollow grind
Use a whetstone grinder to form a hollow grind, which makes creating a clean flat bevel much more achievable; the biggest problem for beginners is rounding over the bevel.

3 Polish by stropping
Stropping regularly is very useful, but it is important not to round over the edge: a wood or MDF strop is recommended, rather than leather, which has too much give and rounds the edge.

UNDERSTANDING A

SPOON KNIFE & SCORP

Both these tools are designed to make concave cuts for carving a hollow. A spoon knife tends to be used on smaller pieces. More power can be put into a scorp as it is employed with both hands, like a drawknife.

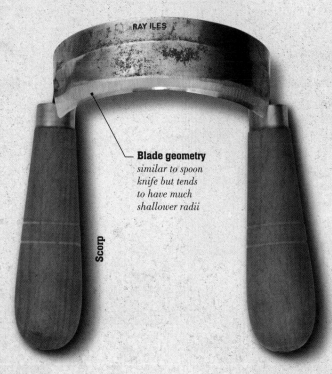

Longer handles
enable levering cuts to be made with both hands

RAY ILES

Blade geometry
similar to spoon knife but tends to have much shallower radii

Scorp

Spoon knife

Safety Tips

Store both tools in protective sheaths when not in use and never walk with blades exposed.

A spoon knife is most commonly employed in thumb pull grip. When carving in this grip it is crucial that your thumb is not in line with the direction of cut: keep it carefully tucked behind the piece instead.

SCORP

■ **Uses** A scorp can be used to hollow large bowls and small shallow dishes. It is also an excellent tool for excavating the indentation of a chair seat.

■ **Efficiency** A scorp is a very efficient hollowing tool, since the blade makes very wide shavings over a large surface area.

■ **Skewing** Just like a drawknife, the scorp can be skewed to take a finer cut.

"SPOON KNIVES CAN ALSO BE CALLED BENT KNIVES BUT ARE NOT CROOKED KNIVES."

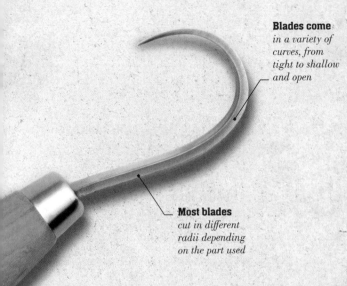

Blades come *in a variety of curves, from tight to shallow and open*

Most blades *cut in different radii depending on the part used*

Spoon Knife

■ **Using on spoons** As the name suggests, spoon knives are commonly used to make concave cuts in spoon carving. As well as the hollow of the bowl, they will also carve a nice concave on the back of the bowl's transition into the neck, or a thumb indentation on the top of the handle.

■ **Other uses** They can also be used to carve the hollow of a cup, add texture to a butter paddle, or refine the interior surface of a bowl. This style of spoon knife with a "question mark" shaped blade is the most adaptable, other more open curves can be useful for shallower cuts.

FOCUS ON...
Attaching the Knife Handle

Some people use the shrinkage of green wood to eventually hold the blade in place. If the knife has a flat cross-section, the space either side in the handle hole can be filled with split pieces of dowel gently tapered, glued, and tapped into place.

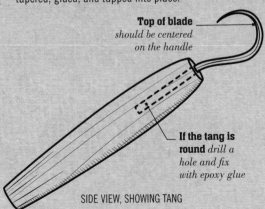

Top of blade *should be centered on the handle*

If the tang is round *drill a hole and fix with epoxy glue*

SIDE VIEW, SHOWING TANG

SHARPEN

Key to sharpening both a spoon knife and scorp is to create a convex blade shape so that the edge does not dig into concave surfaces.

The Geometry

For a clean cut around the inside of a concave, the outside surface must be correspondingly convex. It is easiest to create two or more bevels, which could then be rounded to give control over the shape.

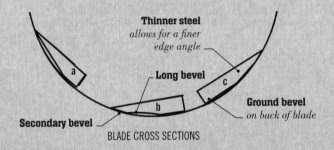

Thinner steel *allows for a finer edge angle*

Long bevel

Ground bevel *on back of blade*

Secondary bevel

a

b

c

BLADE CROSS SECTIONS

a A single long bevel causes the edge to dig into the wood.

b With two bevels, the secondary bevel guides the edge and the long bevel provides shoulders for levering the edge out of the cut.

c Blades made with thinner steel require a wider cross section for strength, and can have a bevel taken off the back.

The Process

1 Work the inside
Sharpen the inside of the blade using wet-and-dry abrasive paper wrapped around a wooden dowel. Saw a fine slot halfway down the dowel for the paper to catch in and wrap around.

2 Work the outside
Sharpen the outside of the blade using a flat board with wet-and-dry paper adhered to it. A diamond stone also works well. Keep control over the bevel length and aim for parallel lines; start with a ¼in (6mm) bevel and a secondary bevel on the very edge.

UNDERSTANDING AN
Ax & Adze

These kindred dual-action tools can be used with force to quickly chop out waste material, or employed more gently to make fairly precise shaping cuts. The rounded blade of a bowl adze makes it suitable for hollowing.

Ax

■ **Chopping cuts** These produce chips and are made at a roughly 30° angle to the surface, slicing through the fibers of the wood and splitting it along the grain.

■ **Shaving cuts** Slicing at a shallower angle engages the bevels to take shavings rather than chips.

■ **Accuracy** With an ax, it is the plane of the swing, adjusted by wrist and arm for accuracy, that defines where the cut occurs.

Good width *at the top end of the handle is useful for flicking cuts*

WOOD TOOLS

Ax

Rounded end *can be held loosely with hooked middle finger, to swing out of cuts*

FOCUS ON...
ATTACHING THE AX HEAD

Fit an axe head by knocking a wedge into the top of the handle through the center of the "eye." To fix a loose head, carefully hammer with a chisel to open up room for the thin end of a wedge, then knock it in to splay the handle so the wood fills the eye. Leave part of the wedge slightly raised for future adjustments. If the eye is an hourglass shape, you can knock the head down lower to compress the fibers for a better fit.

Head loosens *as wood fibers of handle compress*

Wedge pushes *out sides of handle*

BACK VIEW WITH WEDGE CROSS SECTION

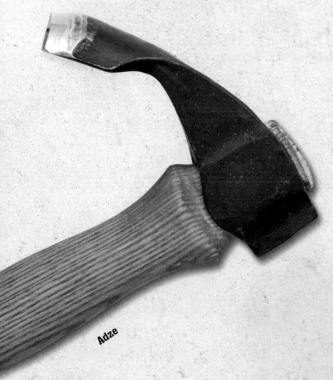

Adze

ADZE

■ **Cutting action** Like the ax, an adze can be used in two modes: chopping and shaving. Unlike an ax, most adzescannot be used to chop down trees or split wood.

■ **Hollowing** The type of small adze with a tight curve shown here is ideal for creating hollows, such as in spoons, bowls, and the seats of chairs.

■ **Accuracy** The adze is a much more accurate tool than an ax because the edge is a fixed length from the pivot point at the handle. Adjusting the pivot point by moving your wrist accurately dictates where the cut will occur.

Safety Tips

Consider the direction of swing in case you follow through: don't put your body in the way!

Consider hand placement when holding the work piece and ensure your technique gives complete control. Beware the ax may bounce off the wood if the edge doesn't bite.

HOW TO

SHARPEN

The cutting edge of an ax is most versatile with two straight bevels. An adze often has a problematic secondary bevel to work on.

The Geometry

Some people advocate a convex bevel on an ax, since it helps direct the blade out of the cut. Flat, short bevels, however, are more suited to general carving because they allow straight, convex, and shallow concave cuts to be taken. With an adze, the main issue is dealing with the steep secondary bevel often left by manufacturers.

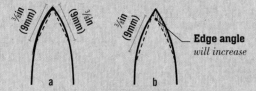

⅜in (9mm)   ⅜in (9mm)   ⅜in (9mm)

Edge angle *will increase*

a   b

AX BLADE CROSS SECTIONS

a Grind two flat ⅜in (9mm) bevels either side of the edge; these are best created with a hollow grind first.

b If two bevels cause the edge to roll or wear too quickly, maintain length on the side predominantly used to make cuts by removing material from the opposite side.

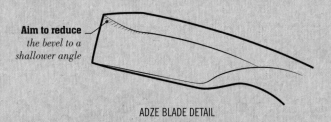

Aim to reduce *the bevel to a shallower angle*

ADZE BLADE DETAIL

The Process

Sharpening an ax
Reshaping can be done with files/angle grinders/grinding belts and dry stone bench grinders, but it is best if the ax is first hollow ground with a motorized whetstone, and the hollow then flattened with a diamond stone.

Grinding an adze
Grind the secondary bevel on the inside of an adze blade with a drum sander attachment on an electric drill.

UNDERSTANDING A
FROE & WEDGE

Cleaving wood is the process of splitting out billets from fresh logs without the use of power tools, and it is the essential starting point of all green woodcraft. After an ax and mallet, a froe and wedge are the next essential tools, increasing your ability to control the split.

The edge
should never be sharp enough to cut fingers

Froe

> **66 ROUNDED EDGES** HELP A WEDGE TO **LAST LONGER.** TOO MANY **SHARP EDGES** WILL MAKE IT PRONE TO **SPLITTING. 99**

FOCUS ON...
ATTACHING THE HANDLE

The handle of the type of froe shown here is fed through a tapering eye. The flared base of the handle allows it to be knocked securely into the eye; the tapering eye compresses the fibres making it stronger. The handle suffers a lot of compression from being hit with a mallet, so it is best to use fast-growing wood, which tends to be strong; look for five growth rings per 1in (25mm).

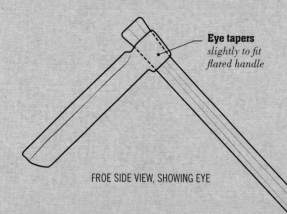

Eye tapers
slightly to fit flared handle

FROE SIDE VIEW, SHOWING EYE

Wedge

Chamfer the
edges *to prevent
damage*

FROE

■ **Controlled splitting** Combined with a cleaving brake,
a froe is extremely effective for controlling splits down
longer, thinner pieces. Hold the piece in a brake and,
with both hands on the froe blade, put tension on the
side where the split should run, then lever the wood
open with your elbow on the end of the froe handle.

■ **Splitting fat logs** A froe is much better suited than
an ax for splitting short, wide logs, which with an ax
would require laborious scoring to split.

WEDGE

■ **Chasing splits** When carved from a tough hardwood,
wedges can be used by themselves to split softer pieces.
More frequently, they are used with a knife, ax, or froe
to hold open splits once started, so that the split may be
chased down the log.

■ **Wood versus metal** A wooden wedge is usually a
much better choice than a metal wedge, since you rarely
want to hit metal on metal. For example, a wooden wedge
can be hit with force by a metal sledgehammer, or placed
next to an ax in a split without fear of damaging the ax.

■ **Power ratio** A thin wedge with a shallow gradient
provides a greater power ratio than a thick wedge,
although it must be driven in deeper to widen the split
the same amount.

▌ Safety Tips

When hitting the froe with a mallet, take
care not to catch the knuckles of your hand
gripping the handle.

Keep fingers outside of the split in case the
split closes. The closing action can have
great force, particularly with bigger logs.

Start slowly when hitting a wedge, since
they can fly out, especially if they are thick.

SHARPEN

*A froe needs to be blunt enough to grip firmly
along the edge without fear of cuts. You may,
however, need to sharpen a secondhand froe.*

The Geometry

A froe does not have a distinct bevel to its blade but it does have
a relatively flat surface that enables it to penetrate wood easily.
A thin edge to the blade, especially on a small froe, will help to
prevent splits from traveling too far.

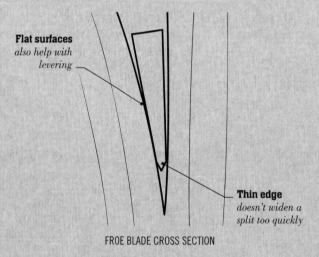

Flat surfaces
*also help with
levering*

Thin edge
*doesn't widen a
split too quickly*

FROE BLADE CROSS SECTION

The Process

Reshaping a secondhand froe

You may find some "mushrooming" of the profile shape
on a secondhand froe because the previous owner used
a metal hammer on it. If this is the case, you can flatten
it and thin back the edge using a file or angle grinder.

Tenon Cutter & Reamer

While tapered tenon joints can be formed with an ax or drawknife and a straight knife, the tools shown here are useful when speed and greater accuracy are required. A tenon cutter shaves the end of a component to a tapered cylinder, while the reamer drills the corresponding tapered mortise hole.

Blades run *down the entire length of the reamer body*

Reamer

■ **Drill or brace** The reamer attachment can be attached to an electric drill or a manual brace. When trying for the first time, it may be best to turn by hand with a brace for greater control.

■ **Steeper gradients** Reamers are available with shallower angles. A finer gradient, typically 1:7, is arguably preferable since the tenon will wedge in place more readily; however, such tenons are more likely to split if hit home too hard.

Mark the depth *to ream to with a felt tip pen*

Reamer

❝ THE CUTTER AND REAMER ARE LIKE POSITIVE AND NEGATIVE IMAGES OF A TAPERED TENON JOINT. ❞

Screws for *adjustments to the blade*

Tenon cutter

Tenon cutter

■ **Cutter sizes** Tenon cutters come in various different sizes, for cutting both tapered and straight tenons. Cutters with diameters of ⅜in (9.5mm) and ⅝in (16mm), both with the same taper, were used for the tapered tenons in this book, and these cover the full range of the reamer shown.

■ **Positioning centrally** When using, it is critical to keep the cutter centered on the end of the component, with an even gap all around between the wood and the cutter.

■ **Using with a vice** By securing the tenon cutter to a workbench with a vise, you can use two hands to turn the component.

■ **Blade adjustments** How the blade is aligned can make a significant difference in how the tenons match the reamed hole. Alignment can be adjusted slightly with an Allen key; it is worth doing a test joint and adjusting.

HOW TO
SHARPEN

To maintain efficiency and accuracy, both the reamer and tenon cutter should be kept properly sharpened.

The Geometry

The cutting blade of a reamer has a simple geometry, and to keep it sharp requires only maintaining the flatness of the bevel. To sharpen the tenon cutter blade, follow the same edge geometry for sharpening a plane; *see* p201.

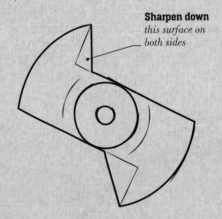

Sharpen down *this surface on both sides*

REAMER OVERHEAD VIEW

The Process

Sharpening the reamer

Rub a small diamond stone evenly over all parts of the blade bevel until completely flat. Some people use a burnisher (a polished, very hard steel rod) to turn a burr on to the edge of a reamer. This is done in a similar way as sharpening a cabinet scraper; *see* p183 for more information on burrs.

Sharpening the tenon cutter

Flatten the back of the blade, then grind the same angle of bevel as for a plane. Hone the microbevel on a diamond stone; a honing guide can be useful for this.

DRAW &
PUSH KNIFE

Two-handled knives make it easy to put your full body strength into cuts, which makes for more efficient shaping. As the names suggest, a drawknife is used by drawing it toward you, and a push knife by pushing it away.

> " A **DRAWKNIFE** SHAVES MORE **QUICKLY** THAN A STRAIGHT KNIFE, AND IS MORE **ACCURATE** THAN AN AX. "

Push knife

Drawknife

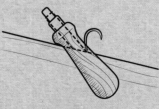

FOCUS ON...

DRAWKNIFE HANDLES

Different styles of drawknife work in different ways. With both, you'll find if they are used the "wrong" way up the edge will dig in too much. Drawknives with cranked handles tend to be used bevel up and those with straight handles work best with the bevel down.

BEVEL UP

BEVEL DOWN

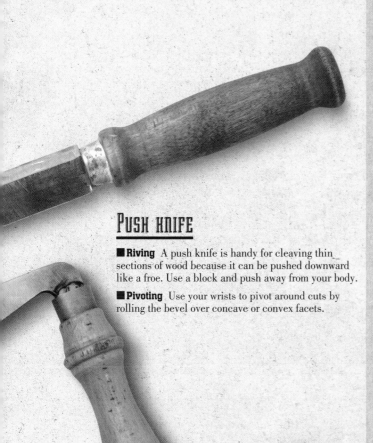

Push knife

■ **Riving** A push knife is handy for cleaving thin sections of wood because it can be pushed downward like a froe. Use a block and push away from your body.

■ **Pivoting** Use your wrists to pivot around cuts by rolling the bevel over concave or convex facets.

Draw knife

■ **Hardware** Most effective on a shaving horse, a drawknife can also be used on wood held in a vise.

■ **Even wear** The center of the long blade tends to get worn down more quickly. Use different parts of the blade for more even wear, and pay attention to any differences when sharpening.

■ **Bevel up or down** A drawknife with a cranked handle and the blade bevel up (*see* left) is better for carving flat surfaces, since there is a longer section of metal in contact with the wood. With the bevel down, you are able to cut concaves and both knives will cut straighter if the blade is skewed.

▌ Safety Tips

Always hold these knives with two hands, both when making cuts and when carrying.

Keep the edge in a fixed position from your body by tucking in elbows and moving your body to effect the cut.

SHARPEN

When sharpening a cranked bevel-up drawknife, use a large diamond stone to flatten the large, flat side of the blade, and a smaller diamond stone for the short bevel.

The Geometry

The final edge angle of a drawknife should be around 30–35°, and that of a push knife should be 25°. Be careful not to lose this geometry when sharpening the blades.

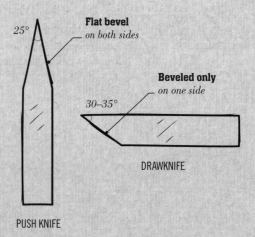

25°

Flat bevel
on both sides

Beveled only
on one side

30–35°

DRAWKNIFE

PUSH KNIFE

The Process

1 Flatten wide back of the drawknife
Use a large diamond stone to achieve a flat surface on the wide section of the blade.

2 Additional bevels
Grinding a secondary bevel or micro bevel on the bevel-up drawknife works well.

3 Hollow grind
Start with a hollow grind for both the push knife and the bevel-down drawknife. They benefit from nicely honed flat bevels started from a hollow grind.

UNDERSTANDING
GOUGES

A gouge is basically a chisel with a curved edge to the blade and often also a curved profile down its length. They are used in relief carving and for shaping hollows both on and off the lathe.

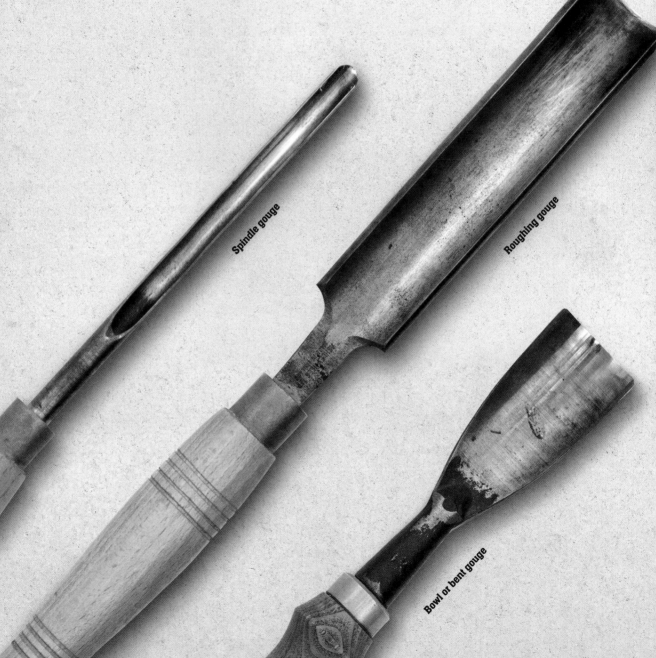

Spindle gouge

Roughing gouge

Bowl or bent gouge

Spindle gouge

■ **Profile** A spindle gouge has a straight profile along its length that enables it to be used for turning.

■ **Uses** Use to countersink drilled holes. In turning, spindle gouges are used to shape details, in particular coves. They are also useful for squaring ends, especially when there is a lot of material to remove.

Roughing gouge

■ **Profile** Like the spindle, a roughing gouge also has a straight profile along its length.

■ **Uses** Use in the initial stages of turning to remove bulk. Also useful for creating concave cuts.

Bowl or bent gouge

■ **Profile** A bowl gouge has a curved profile along its length so that it is capable of carving hollows.

■ **Uses** As the name suggest, a bowl gouge is used to carve out hollows, such as for bowls. Also useful for trimming the wedges used to hold legs on carved seats.

▶ Safety Tips

Store gouge blades in protective sheaths when not in use. Keeping them in a tool roll is also helpful.

When using never place your hand or body in front of the cutting edge.

FOCUS ON...
Attaching the handle

Gouges designed to be hit with a mallet often have a ferrule at the end of the handle to keep the fibers together. The best gouges tend be socketed with a shoulder-like bolster that prevents the tang splitting open the handle when the tool is struck.

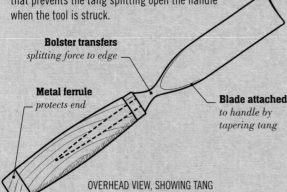

Bolster transfers *splitting force to edge*

Metal ferrule *protects end*

Blade attached *to handle by tapering tang*

OVERHEAD VIEW, SHOWING TANG

HOW TO
Sharpen

Each type of gouge has a different cutting edge geometry that needs to be shaped in contrasting ways to keep them sharp.

The Geometry

Hone flat the bevel of a roughing gouge. A fingernail profile that takes the bevel further down one side is best for a spindle gouge. This produces a large edge, which can be used for skewed cuts and also gives greater access to the tip for tight cuts. The bevel of a bowl gouge is the same as a spoon knife: a gradual convex from the edge; *see p187*.

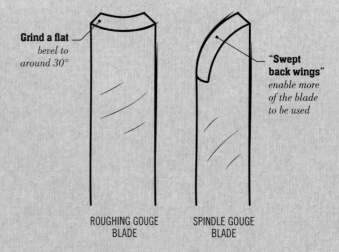

Grind a flat *bevel to around 30°*

"Swept back wings" *enable more of the blade to be used*

ROUGHING GOUGE BLADE   SPINDLE GOUGE BLADE

The Process

Sharpening roughing and bowl gouges
Both gouges are best ground on the whetstone grinder then honed flat; the techniques described in the sharpening section with the tool and diamond stone flat on the bench, work very well. Flatten the cannel with a slipstone or abrasive paper around a dowel.

Sharpening a spindle gouge
Work a spindle gouge on a bench stone. This allows you to roll the gouge around on the stone to hit all parts, while sighting down the bevel.

UNDERSTANDING
CHISELS

Chisels are key tools for removing excess wood precisely and quickly. With the edge at right angles to the handle, cuts are effected by pushing in line with the handle. In joinery, the flat back of a chisel is the foundation of the joints holding our furniture and homes together.

SHEW

■ **Skewed angle** The angle at the end of the bevel is skewed rather than straight.

■ **Relief carving and turning** The skewed end can get into nooks and crannies; for the same reason they are good for turning. Tools for turning are often of stronger steel, however, and relief carving tools could be dangerous on a lathe. Both types of tools rely on their bevels to guide cuts; usually those for relief carving have longer bevels for paring.

■ **Use both hands** With the piece of wood you are working on secured, you can have both hands on the chisel—this triangulates the movement, giving you greater control.

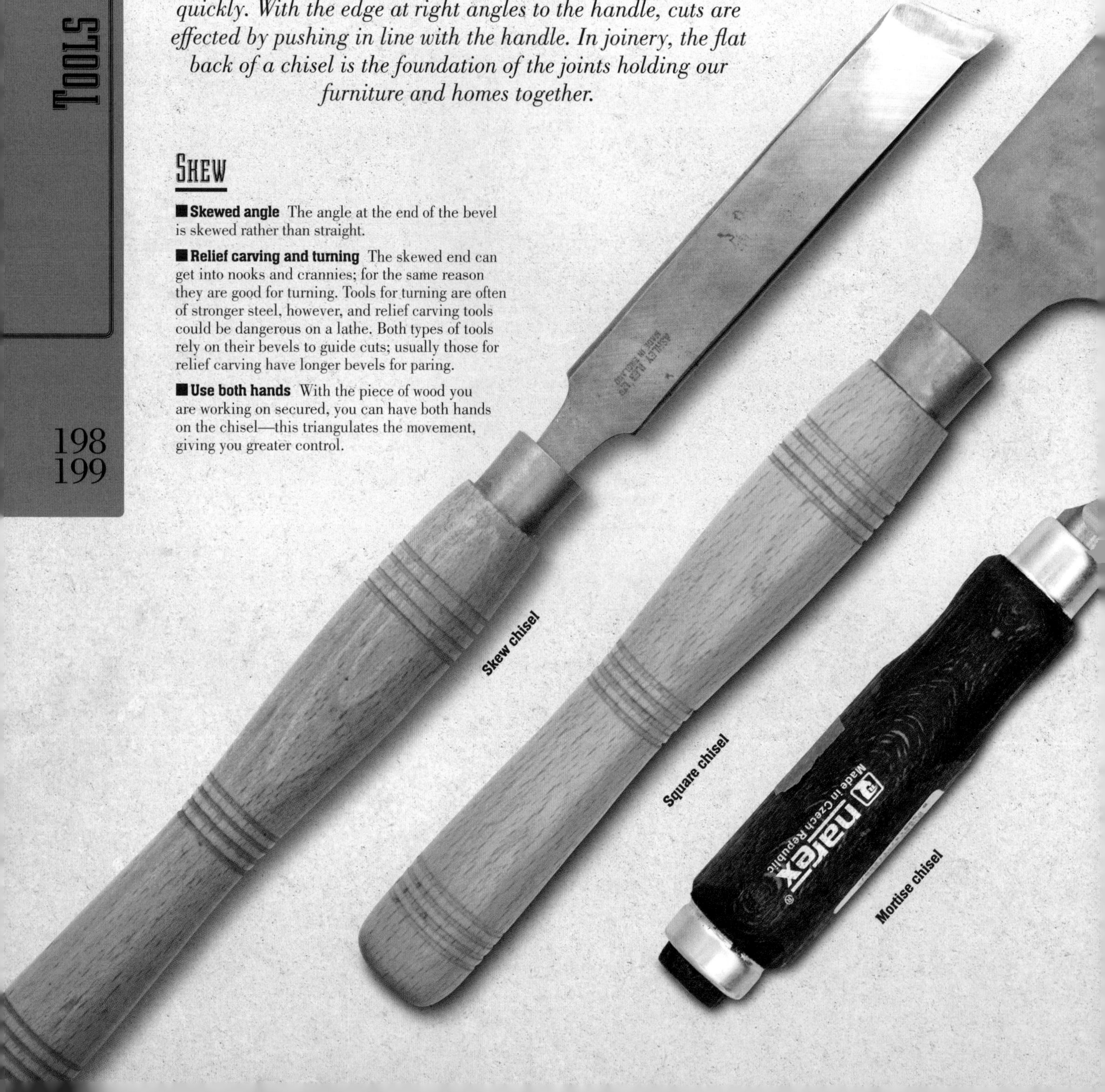

Skew chisel

Square chisel

Mortise chisel

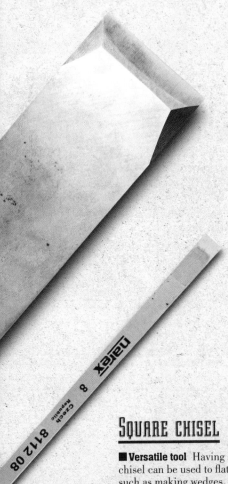

SQUARE CHISEL

■ **Versatile tool** Having such a wide flat blade, this chisel can be used to flatten surfaces and for paring, such as making wedges.

■ **Corners may be taken off** You may wish to file off the corners, because, when used in turning, they have a tendency to scratch the surface of the spindle when the chisel is lifted to take a clean cut with the bevel in contact with the wood.

MORTISE CHISEL

■ **Used for cutting mortises** The size of the chisel determines the width of the mortise.

■ **Deep blade** This allows the sides to rub against the inside edge of the mortise to guide a square cut.

■ **May need reinforcing** If the end of the chisel is being hit, it may need a metal ferrule and either a bolster or socket, to withstand heavy use.

▮ Safety Tips

Can be very dangerous—put protective guards on the ends when not in use.

Hold with both hands if not using a mallet; it can be helpful to place one hand on the end of the handle, against your body, and the other around the main body of the handle.

With a mortise chisel, you are relying on the long flat back to guide the cut, and the bevels are usually there to generate a sharp edge.

The Geometry

A secondary bevel can be particularly useful on a mortise chisel, and makes sharpening easier. Skews and square chisels used for turning, as in this book, should be sharpened with a hollow grind, so the bevel can rest against the curve of the turned billet.

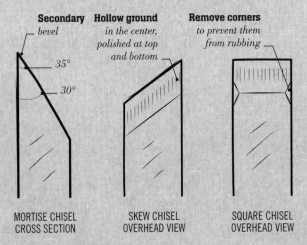

Secondary bevel — 35° — 30°

Hollow ground in the center, polished at top and bottom

Remove corners to prevent them from rubbing

MORTISE CHISEL CROSS SECTION   SKEW CHISEL OVERHEAD VIEW   SQUARE CHISEL OVERHEAD VIEW

The Process

1 Flatten the back of the blade
It is worth putting effort in to make the long section of the chisel, on the other side from the bevel, entirely flat; Japanese waterstones and diamond stones are the most effective ways of achieving this. Once flat, it will need very little work beyond removing the burr from honing the bevel.

2 Hone primary and secondary bevels
Use a honing guide to help you as you sharpen the secondary bevel. Because the secondary bevel is shorter, it will take less time to sharpen.

UNDERSTANDING

PLANES

Planes are used to reduce the thickness of boards, eliminate uneven surfaces, and create a smooth finish. They are particularly useful for shaving flat and true surfaces from which to set a datum face and edge.

Wood scrub plane

66 AS YOU **GLIDE** THE PLANE OVER THE WOOD, THE **ANGLED** **BLADE** SHAVES THE SURFACE TO A **UNIFORM** FINISH. **99**

Unscrew *the lever cap to release the blade assembly*

Jack plane, overhead view

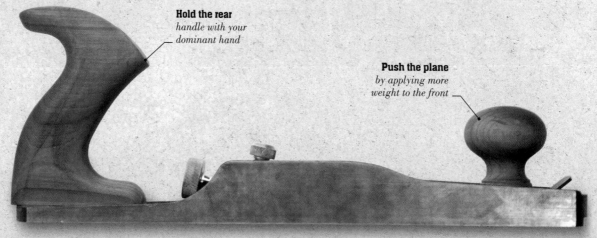

Hold the rear *handle with your dominant hand*

Push the plane *by applying more weight to the front*

Jack plane, side view

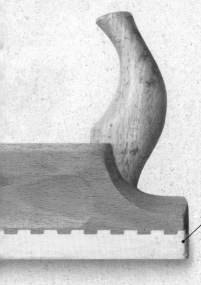

The sole or base *is made from very durable hardwood*

SCRUB PLANE

■ **Cambered blade** The scrub plane has a cambered, or slightly convex, blade, which allows it to make very thick shavings. This is particularly useful when you need to quickly remove waste material in order to flatten a warped surface.

■ **Aggressive cutting** A scrub plane can make very aggressive cuts because it is thin and short; if it were very wide and long it would only be able to take off the very highest points.

■ **Hold the same direction** It is best to move the scrub plane in the same direction. If you try to come at 90° to a board that has already been scrubbed, you will only nibble at the peaks of the furrows; by maintaining cuts in the same direction, you can take full-length shavings all along the tip of each furrow.

■ **Cut across the grain** If the wood you are working on does not have a predictable straight grain, go across the grain with the plane; a diagonal direction is often most efficient.

JACK PLANE

■ **Low-angled cutting** The low-angle, adjustable-mouth jack plane (#5) shown here has a blade that hits wood at an acute angle. While this causes it to dig into difficult grain more readily, it has the benefit of working well on end grain, which higher angled planes struggle with.

■ **Adjustable mouth** The mouth of a jack plane can be opened and closed. When narrowed, the mouth applies pressure in front of the shaving which prevents fibers from splitting ahead of the edge. Open up the mouth to make thicker shavings.

▮ **Safety Tip**

When disassembling and reassembling the plane for sharpening, hold the blade from behind and don't bring your hand too close to the cutting edge.

SHARPEN

A razor sharp plane iron sings as it cuts. Planes need to be correctly set up with clean flat soles, appropriately open mouths, and blades adjusted for the job in hand.

The Geometry

A mortise chisel benefits from having a microbevel ground into the tip of the blade; *see* p181. Blades held at a steep angle tend to make cleaner cuts. If you are struggling with a shallow-angled blade, grinding a 2° secondary bevel effectively steepens the blade angle.

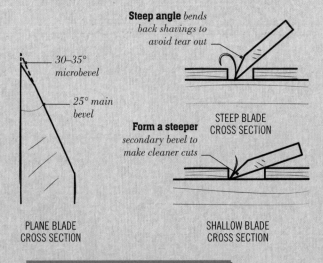

Steep angle *bends back shavings to avoid tear out*

30–35° microbevel

25° main bevel

Form a steeper *secondary bevel to make cleaner cuts*

STEEP BLADE CROSS SECTION

PLANE BLADE CROSS SECTION

SHALLOW BLADE CROSS SECTION

The Process

1 Grind the primary bevel
Remove the blade and grind it to the correct angle on a grinding wheel, or by hand on a coarse bench stone. Continuously move the blade while grinding.

2 Maintain a flat polished surface
Polish the back with Japanese waterstones. Ensure the abrasive is perfectly flat; avoid rounding the edge.

3 Hone a secondary bevel
Check for a bur evenly along the length of the edge, then remove the bur with finer abrasives. It can be helpful to gently radius the final distance towards the corners of the blade, to prevent the corners digging in.

UNDERSTANDING A
FRAME SAW

A frame saw allows you to use a small blade, which is very useful to reduce friction compared to the wide blade of a handsaw. Once the windlass has been tightened, the saw is very sturdy. The thin blade also enables the saw to cut curves, and can be used instead of a bandsaw.

Hooked ends
keep the tension-providing string held in place

" WITH THE CORRECT **BLADE** THE **FRAME SAW** REALLY COMES INTO ITS OWN. "

Split pins with washers *hold an old bandsaw blade in place*

FOCUS ON...
TYPES OF BLADES

The more "teeth per inch" along a saw blade, the smoother the cut, as a rule. Blades with larger teeth are used to remove material fast, but may leave a rough-hewn surface.

Large teeth
with wide gaps take out more material

LOW TPI

Small teeth
with narrow gaps leave a smoother finish

HIGH TPI

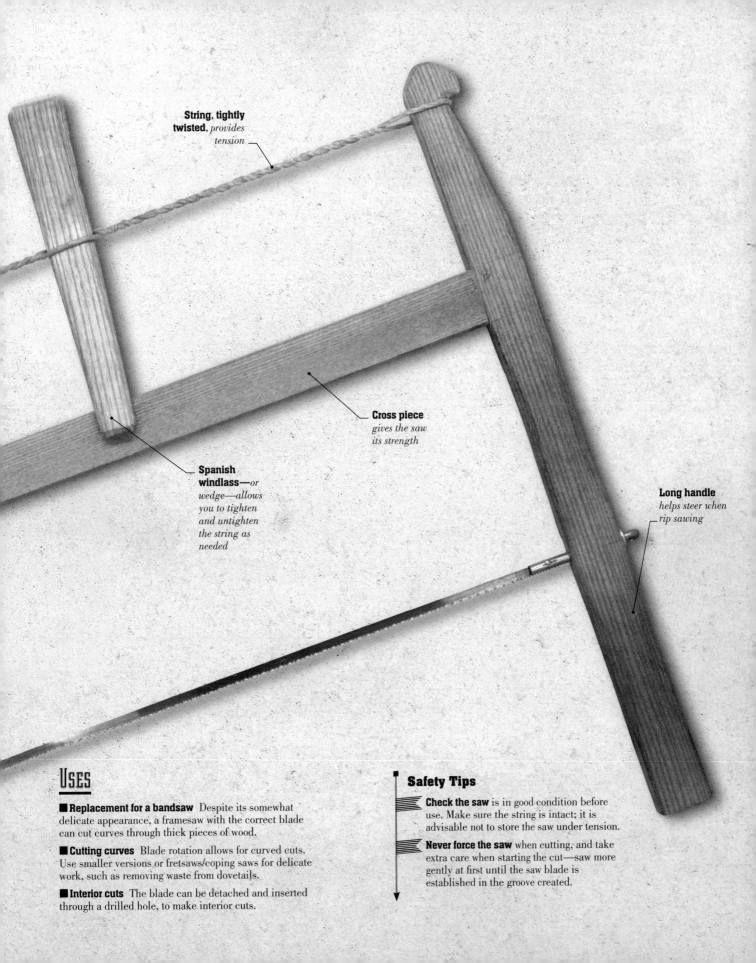

String, tightly twisted, *provides tension*

Cross piece *gives the saw its strength*

Spanish windlass—*or wedge—allows you to tighten and untighten the string as needed*

Long handle *helps steer when rip sawing*

USES

■ **Replacement for a bandsaw** Despite its somewhat delicate appearance, a framesaw with the correct blade can cut curves through thick pieces of wood.

■ **Cutting curves** Blade rotation allows for curved cuts. Use smaller versions or fretsaws/coping saws for delicate work, such as removing waste from dovetails.

■ **Interior cuts** The blade can be detached and inserted through a drilled hole, to make interior cuts.

Safety Tips

Check the saw is in good condition before use. Make sure the string is intact; it is advisable not to store the saw under tension.

Never force the saw when cutting, and take extra care when starting the cut—saw more gently at first until the saw blade is established in the groove created.

UNDERSTANDING

Handsaws

It is useful to have a variety of handsaws at your disposal to tackle the range of shapes and thicknesses of material you may have to saw. The blade size, as well as the size, number, and shape of the teeth, will determine a saw's best uses.

Hacksaw

244

Handsaw

" HOWEVER MUCH **FORCE** YOU PUT IN, SAWING **STEADY** AND **STRAIGHT** IS ALWAYS **FASTEST! "**

Japanese pull saw (Ryoba)

Folding arborist's saw

HACKSAW

■ **A fine-toothed saw** with a metal frame, used for cutting small pieces of metal, such as threaded bars or bandsaw blades.

■ **Not very useful** for the woodworker, generally.

HANDSAW

■ **As the name suggests**, a multipurpose tool, useful for both crosscutting and ripping.

■ **For sawing green wood**, chose a saw with large teeth (such as 7tpi), since they do not clog up with waste wood as readily as smaller-toothed blades.

■ **Cuts on the push stroke** so be careful not to allow the blade to buckle.

■ **Aim for steady, straight cuts**—think of your forearm as only moving in one place, then line up your body to put some extra strength into the action.

JAPANESE PULL SAW

■ **A multipurpose carpentry saw** with two cutting edges, one for ripping and one for crosscutting.

■ **Great for cutting joints**, as well as for general-purpose sawing, giving a neater surface on the cut.

■ **You can also buy** saws with reinforced spines—the spine can cause the saw to get stuck on larger pieces of wood or boards, but it does hold the wood nice and straight for accuracy when sawing tenons, for instance.

FOLDING ARBORIST'S SAW

■ **Perfect for green woodworking**, as they are designed for arborists who work mostly with wet wood.

■ **Very efficient at cutting** through wood, and available in a variety of sizes.

■ **Convenient for carrying** and storing, as they come in their own ready-made sheath—this one is a great size for stuffing into a small pack.

Safety Tips

Secure the wood being sawed with clamps, to stop it moving around as you cut.

Store saws in protective sleeves, both to protect the blade and to avoid causing injuries.

Beware the saw jumping out of the cut: keep your hand out of harm's way.

Plan for the bit of wood that you are cutting off, especially if it is a large log.

DRILLS & DRILL BITS

There are a large number of different types of drill bits, each one suited to a specific purpose. Battery-powered drills are very useful, particularly for small holes and for speed, but the traditional tools are still best for certain jobs: for depth accuracy you can't beat counting the turns of a brace and bit.

Brace

Auger

BRACE

■ **Chuck jaws** The brace has V-shaped blocks to clamp on to the tapered shank of bits. Modern braces can have different chucks: make sure the bits you use match the chuck on the brace or drill.

■ **Rounded handle** The handle can be braced against your body to add stability. If the lead screws are good then the bit should draw itself through the wood without much force from behind.

AUGER

■ **Spurs cut a circular hole** An auger is a useful tool for drilling larger holes—though some claim the spurs can drag across the end grain and distort the hole into an oval shape.

■ **Bullnose auger** Shown here, the bullnose auger cuts extremely well and is useful for drilling into end grain, as well as widening holes and drilling into wood at an angle.

■ **Scotch pattern** A common eye auger; this type is easy to sharpen; it relies on a strong lead screw, particularly if going into end grain.

Safety Tips

▶ **Wear protective gear** and never point a drill at a person.

◀ **Do not touch the bit** after using an electric drill—it will be hot.

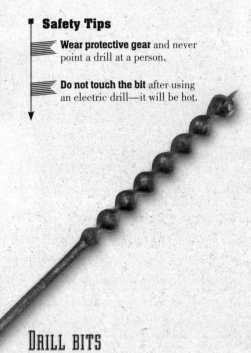

DRILL BITS

■ **Brad-point bit** This bit cuts cleanly, and can be used in a brace: if the lead screw is good you can achieve very accurate depths by counting the number of turns of the brace.

■ **Extenders increase accuracy** An extender increases the distance between hole and drill, which helps with sighting, increasing accuracy, and for lining up holes over distances.

■ **Other specialist bits** Bits specially designed for cutting wood (including thin and flat bits), for cutting metal, and for use in masonry are available. Flat bits are less useful for tough woods metal; twist drill bits work fine for small holes in wood.

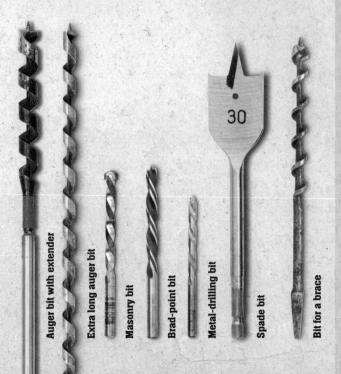

Auger bit with extender | Extra long auger bit | Masonry bit | Brad-point bit | Metal-drilling bit | Spade bit | Bit for a brace

HOW TO
SHARPEN

Do not sharpen the outside of augers and drill bits, as this will change the shape and size of the hole the tool cuts.

The Geometry

The "lip," or "cutter," of the auger should be kept sharp. If there is a raised spur on the very end of the cutting lip—sometimes known as a "nicker"—it should also be sharpened. If damaged, the lead screw can be restored with a needle file or small triangular file.

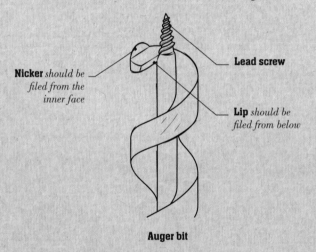

Nicker *should be filed from the inner face*

Lead screw

Lip *should be filed from below*

Auger bit

The Process

1 File the cutting edges
A diamond file is a good choice for achieving a polished cutting edge on an auger or drill bit. For some bits a small triangular file may be best.

2 Use a round file on concave surfaces
If sharpening concave sections of an auger or drill bit—such as the inside of the end of a bullnose auger—use a round file.

3 Use a grinding wheel
A simple metal twist drill bit is best sharpened on a grinding wheel.

UNDERSTANDING
MEASURING TOOLS

Along with the standard long metal ruler and sharp pencil, there are a number of highly useful measuring tools that should be part of a woodworker's arsenal. Accurate measuring is the foundation of joinery. Take good care of your measuring tools—and double-check everything!

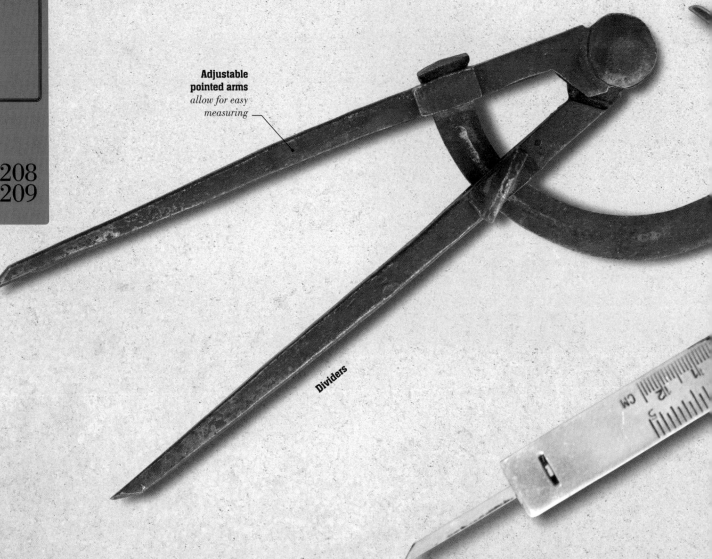

Adjustable pointed arms *allow for easy measuring*

Dividers

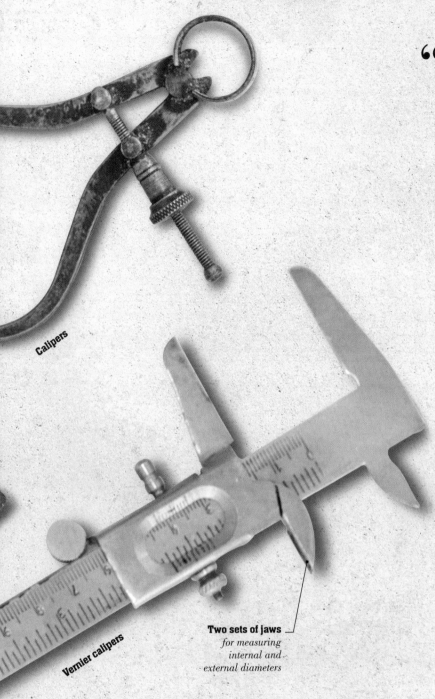

Calipers

Vernier calipers

Two sets of jaws _for measuring internal and external diameters_

CALIPERS

■ **Used to measure** diameters; this style is used specifically for external diameters, such as the thickness of a table leg, but they also come designed to measure internal diameters, and sometimes both.

■ **Check measurements quickly** by simply setting the calipers to the diameter of the object being measured, then holding them against a ruler (or vice versa).

■ **Useful for checking** diameters when turning spindles or bowls on a lathe.

DIVIDERS

■ **As the name suggests**, these can be very useful for dividing up spaces, particularly when not on a straight line.

■ **Quickly and efficiently** mark with the pointed ends, which can stay put as you swivel the dividers around, meaning there is less chance of error.

■ **Good for scoring curves** into boards or blanks, when used like a pair of compasses.

■ **Measure awkward** three-dimensional objects, such as the distance between the base of a chair's seat and a specific part of one of its legs.

VERNIER CALIPERS

■ **Useful for transferring measurements**, just like other calipers, but with the benefit of increased accuracy thanks to the Vernier scale.

■ **Internal and external jaws** can both be used to measure widths and thicknesses, and the stem can also be used to measure depths—particularly useful for measuring drilled holes.

■ **Jaws can be locked** to further reduce the chance of mistakes while transfering measurements.

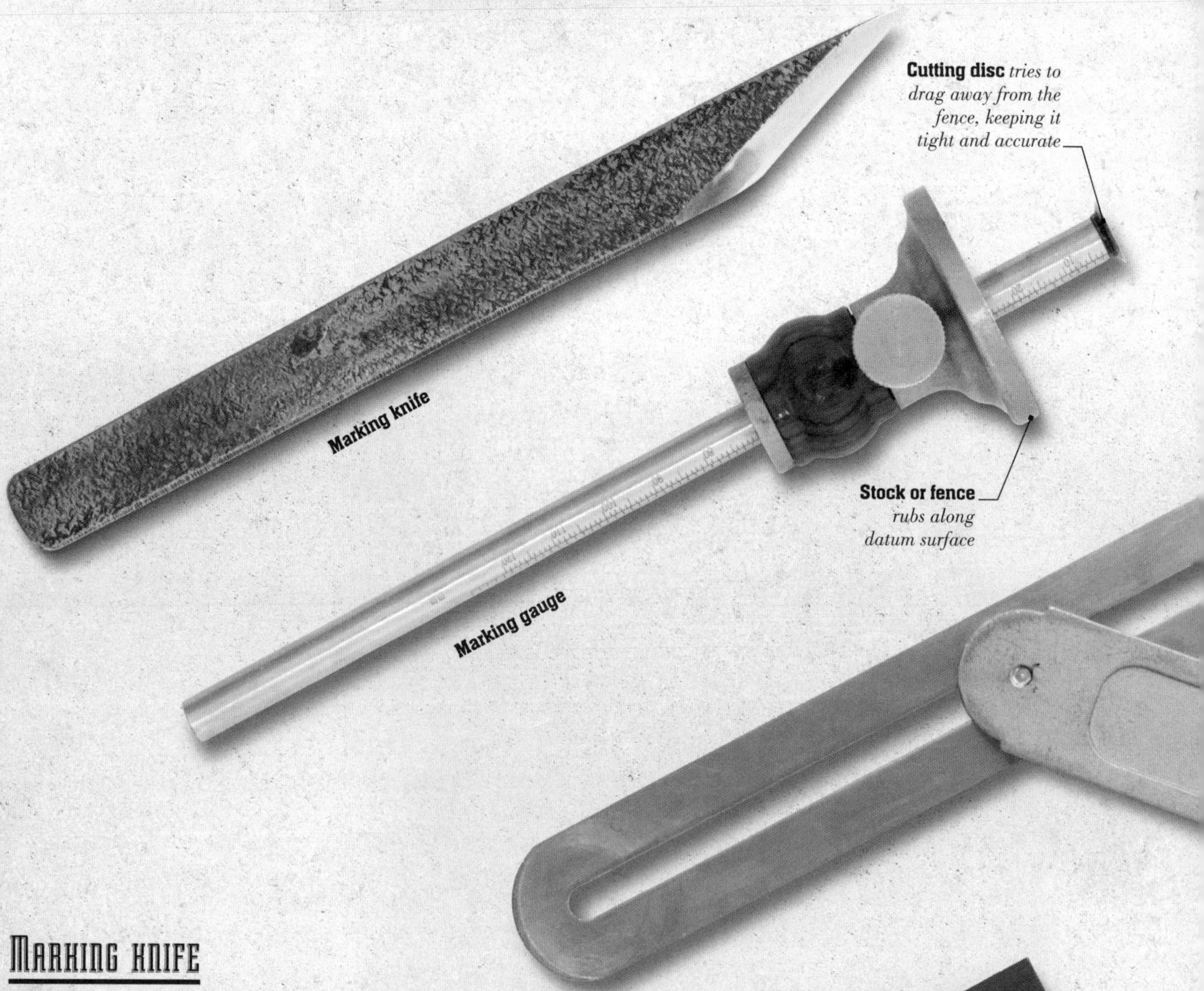

Cutting disc *tries to drag away from the fence, keeping it tight and accurate*

Marking knife

Marking gauge

Stock or fence *rubs along datum surface*

Try square

MARKING KNIFE

■ **Align against a ruler** Use instead of a pencil for effective, accurate marking out—the sharp point is more precise.

■ **Transfer measurements quickly** Measurements can be transfered easily, for instance when making dovetail pins straight from the tails.

■ **Asymmetric grind** The blade is drawn toward the datum, which is beneficial for accuracy.

MARKING GAUGE

■ **Scribes an accurate line** The marking gauge scores an accurate line from a given datum surface, which can then be drawn in with a pencil or cut with a knife—but remember that this line will only be as accurate as the datum it was measured from.

■ **Adjustable headstock** Measure a range of distances.

■ **Wheel scores line** Other variations, such as those that score with a pin or knife, are available, but the wheel works particularly well running along the grain as it tends not to follow the fibers as much as other types.

Cover the blade of a marking knife when not in use.

Keep fingers out of harm's way.

Sliding bevel

SLIDING BEVEL

■ **Adjustable arm** Sliding bevels can measure any angle.

■ **"Locking screw"** keeps the angle in place, and is located in an unobstrusive place on this Japanese model.

■ **Used like a try square** The sliding bevel can be used in the same way as a try square.

TRY SQUARE

■ **There are two parts**: the stock and the blade. This one has a wooden stock with a brass face plate to keep it true. It is designed to be used on solid three-dimensional objects: the stock rests against a datum surface and the blade is used to cut or draw a line at 90° to it.

■ **Three brass bolts** Bolts hold the two pieces together.

■ **Test for trueness** Line the try square up with a known straight edge and draw a square line on it, then flip the try square and draw another line—if the square is accurate, the two lines should be parallel.

HOW TO

SHARPEN

The marking knife must have a flat side so that it can sit accurately against the rule or square. Orienting the bevel this way guides it towards the rule, making sure that it doesn't get dragged off course by the grain.

The Geometry

A Japanese marking knife with a forged hollow on the inside makes it quick to flatten when sharpening. It is important that one side of the blade is flat, as it should rest against the side of a ruler when you are measuring and marking out.

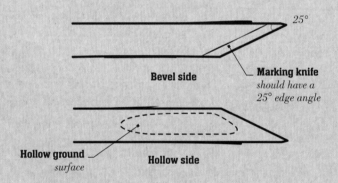

25°

Bevel side

Marking knife
*should have a
25° edge angle*

Hollow ground
surface

Hollow side

The Process

Grind one side of a marking knife flat

A marking knife needs to have one side perfectly flat, to ensure accurate measurements. A diamond stone is a good choice of abrasive to achieve this.

Sharpen the disc of a marking gauge

If your marking gauge has a wheel, unscrew the disc and rub it on a diamond stone, or any other flat abrasive, to sharpen it.

File the points of dividers

Use a fine file or stone to sharpen the two points of dividers, as it is useful for the ends to be sharp.

CHAPTER 05

HARDWARE

Nothing is more satisfying than creating your own wood-crafting hardware from scratch. Tailor-make your equipment to suit your needs and take your craft to the next level.

MAKE A
SHAVING HORSE

A shaving horse is effectively a workbench, clamp, and seat combined into a single piece of hardware, adapted for efficient working with a draw knife: the harder you pull, the stronger the clamping force from your legs.

YOU WILL NEED

TOOLS & EQUIPMENT

- Pencil, marking knife, and measuring equipment
- Ax and ax block
- ⅝in (16mm) tenon cutter
- Straight knife
- Sliding bevel
- Electric drill with ⅝in (16mm) bit and ⅝in (16mm) reamer
- Frame saw and pull saw
- Mortise chisel and mallet
- Hammer and safety goggles

MATERIALS

- For the legs: 4 x billets of green wood, trued to about 2⅜in (60mm) x 20in (508mm)
- For other pieces: scaffolding planks 3ft 10in x 8⅞ x 1⁷⁄₁₆in (3m x 225 x 36mm), sawn into sections indicated below
- For pegs: 1 green wood log, about 2⅜in (60mm) diameter and 10¼in (260mm) long
- For the arm pin: mild steel rod, ⅜in (9mm) wide and 13in (330mm) long
- Bolts and washers
- 3⅛in (80mm) wood screws
- Wood glue and swizzle stick

SKILLS

REMIND YOURSELF HOW TO

- Shape with an ax: *p50*
- Form a tapered tenon: *pp56, 130*
- Use a tenon cutter: *p130*
- Use a reamer: *p130*
- Use a chisel: *p118*
- Peg joints: *p130*
- Level legs: *p154*

KNIFE GRIPS

- Chest lever: *p19*
- Thumb push: *p22*
- Shin pull: *p63*
- Thumb pull: *p21*

DESIGN GUIDE

Based on a traditional "dumbhead" style, we have kept this design very simple and cheap. To use it, you push the treadle forwards with your feet to bring the swinging arm down towards the platform, thereby clamping the billet with the head. Longer billets can be placed along either side of the arm, and the angled platform enables efficient shaving action.

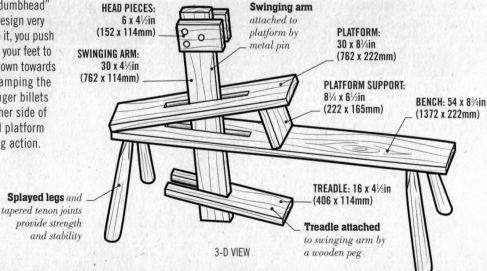

HEAD PIECES: 6 x 4½in (152 x 114mm)

Swinging arm *attached to platform by metal pin*

SWINGING ARM: 30 x 4½in (762 x 114mm)

PLATFORM: 30 x 8¾in (762 x 222mm)

PLATFORM SUPPORT: 8¾ x 6½in (222 x 165mm)

BENCH: 54 x 8¾in (1372 x 222mm)

Splayed legs *and tapered tenon joints provide strength and stability*

TREADLE: 16 x 4½in (406 x 114mm)

Treadle attached *to swinging arm by a wooden peg*

3-D VIEW

> **❝ A TENON CUTTER IS IN ESSENCE JUST A LARGE PENCIL SHARPENER. ❞**

The Process

1 Rough taper the leg tenons

Using an ax, cut a tapered tenon on each leg piece. Draw a circle slightly larger than the thin end of the tenon, in the center at one end; you could draw around a small coin. Start the taper far down the leg and chop angled facets all the way around; *see* Tip, above. Cut a square around the circle mark, then take off the corners with finer cuts until it is roughly circular.

Techniques: Shaping with an ax, forming a tapered tenon—see pp50, 56

Blend in *the shoulder until smooth and even*

2 Finish the tapers

Test fit the tenon cutter: any areas where it isn't fitting will show with scuff marks. Shave these down with a knife in chest lever grip. Once it fits, twist the tenon cutter around the end to create a perfect taper, making sure the tenon stays centered. If the cutter creates a shoulder, remove it with a knife in thumb push grip.

Technique: Using a tenon cutter— see p130

Knife grip: Chest lever, thumb push—see pp19, 22

Angling the Reamer

Remember to account for the reamer's taper, either try to sight straight down the center of the reamer, or adjust the sliding bevel so that you can sight the outside of the reamer, aligned with the sliding bevel.

For example, our reamer has a 6.4° taper (or 12.8° included angle, i.e. the angles on both sides of the reamer combined), so you need to adjust the sliding bevel by the same amount, adding 6.4° degrees to it.

Place a scrap piece *underneath to avoid breakout*

3 Drill the leg mortises
On what will be the underside of the platform, mark the mortise hole positions for the leg tenons, 5in (127mm) from the end and 2in (51mm) from the sides. Draw sight lines for each hole at 45° and set a sliding bevel to 15° for the angle of splay. With the section resting on ax blocks or a workbench, drill the holes right through. Get someone to help you sight it straight and at the correct angle, or use a mirror.

4 Ream the leg mortises
Taper the mortises to match the leg tenons by drilling them with a reamer cutting attachment. Make sure you are drilling at the correct angle, ideally with some help sighting as you drill; *see* above. Drill to the full depth of the reamer so as to make the largest and strongest joint possible.

Technique: Using a reamer attachment—see p130

CONTINUED ☞

TIP
Scoring the pencil guidelines with a marking knife creates a groove to help the saw and chisel blades cut accurately.

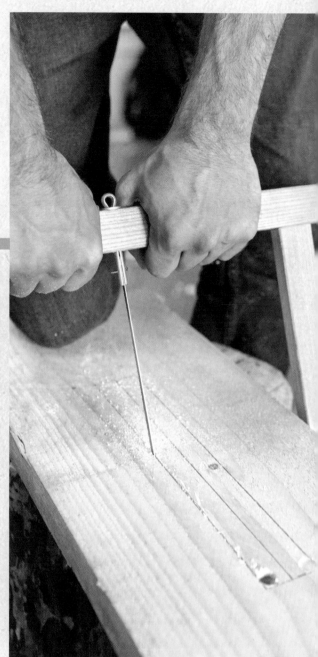

5 Mark slots for the swinging arm

Mark slots for the swinging arm on the bench and platform sections. Draw a line down the middle of each, starting 11in (279mm) from one end for both sections, but extend the line to 14in (356mm) on the bench and only 12in (305mm) on the platform. Mark the width of the slots, centered on these lines and equivalent to the thickness of the plank with 1/32in (1mm) leeway on either side. Go over the lines with a marking knife to score in the edges.

6 Saw the long edges

Drill access holes in each corner of one end of a slot, wide enough to fit a frame saw blade. Insert the blade, make sure it's correctly angled and fixed, then saw straight down a long edge. Swap sides and repeat. If using a turning saw then turn it to take the short cut between the two long ones; if you can't with the saw you could use a chisel.

7 Chisel the ends

Chisel out a section at one of the short ends of the slot. Hold the chisel perpendicular and hit the end of the handle with a mallet to cut out a chip, then tilt the chisel to lever out the chip. Repeat to cut across the width of the slot. Chip out another section, then remove more layers, progressively deeper, until you cut right through. Repeat at the opposite end until the slot falls out, then clean up any ragged edges with the chisel. Repeat for the other slot.

Technique: Using a chisel—see p118

Chipping out
a second section gives clearance to the blade

8 Form the platform support

Take the platform support piece and, in the center at one end, mark and saw out a tenon 3⅛in (80mm) wide and as deep as the plank thickness. Hold the tenon against the platform to mark a corresponding mortise. First draw a guideline 2⅜in (60mm) back from the end closest to the slot, then line the tenon up to it and draw around. Score the guidelines with a marking knife and chisel out the slot as described in step 7.

CONTINUED ☞

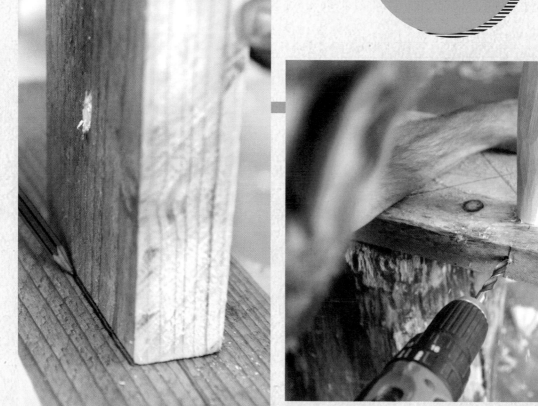

9 Cut the treadle slot

Mark the slot in the treadle for the arm by drawing a center line, marking a point 8in (203mm) from one end, placing the swinging arm vertically centered at this point, and then drawing around it to set the width. Saw along these lines, then chisel it out as in step 7.

Hold the treadle
secure on a block or other work surface as you saw

10 Attach a leg

Spread glue around the inside of a leg mortise with a swizzle stick or wood shaving, then bang in the leg. Draw a line across the side of the bench at the angle of splay, centered along the tenon. Mark a point a bit less than halfway up this line, so there is plenty of tenon to drill into and enough of the body plank for strength. Drill a ⅜in (10mm) hole, straight on all planes and to the full length of the bit, through the bench and leg tenon.

MAKING THE LEG PEGS

Cleave two billets from a quartersawn section of the log and rough shape them with an ax to about $^{13}/_{16}$in (20mm) square.

Holding the billet in the middle, use a knife in shin pull grip to first round one side to $^3/_8$in (10mm), then taper its end to $^5/_{16}$in (8mm).

Repeat on the other side and saw the billet in two. Finally, use thumb pull grip to chamfer the wider ends, to protect them from splitting when they are hammered.

11 Peg the leg

Draw a pencil line on a peg to the depth of the hole just drilled and spread glue around the thinner end. Insert the peg by hand, then knock it in with a hammer until the pencil line is buried in the hole; the sound of the hammer should change pitch once it is all the way in. Saw off the peg waste. Repeat for the other legs and adjust their heights so that the horse sits level at about 19$^{11}/_{16}$in (500mm) from the top of the seat to the floor.

Techniques: Pegging joints, leveling legs—see pp130, 154

12 Peg the treadle and arm

Place the arm into the treadle slot with the treadle ever so slightly angled, as in the photo of the finished horse; you are aiming to drill through the center of the arm around 3in (76mm) from the bottom. Drill a ½in (12mm) hole through one side of the treadle, enough to mark the arm, then take them apart and continue drilling both separately, so that you can push a peg through the arm and both sides of the treadle.

Leave the peg *sticking out so that the treadle position can be adjusted*

CONTINUED ☞

TIP

To drill consistent holes in both head pieces, clamp them together and drill all the way through.

13 Drill the head pieces

Place a head piece 1in (25mm) from the top of the swinging arm and draw a guideline along its top edge. Mark positions on the head piece for the three bolt holes: two 1in (25mm) in from the corners of a short edge, the third between these two and then 3½in (89mm) from the rear edge (*see* right). Drill holes all the way through both head pieces using a drill bit the same diameter as your bolts.

14 Bolt head to the arm and bend the pin

Place a head piece back on the arm, lined up with the guideline drawn in step 13. Insert the drill through the holes and use it to mark the bolt hole positions on the arm. Remove the head and drill holes all the way through the arm, then bolt the head pieces tightly into position. For added strength you could glue them, but you may need to replace the head from time to time, so the bolts bring flexibility. Put on safety googles to hammer one end of the metal pin against the edge of an ax block, to form a bent handle.

Make sure
*the screws are
not raised*

15 **Attach the metal pin**
Drill ⅜in (10mm) holes for the metal pin through the center of the side of the platform, 10in (254mm) from the mortise end. It is important to drill straight, so draw guidelines and drill in two stages: first with a thinner bit through to the slot, marking the hole on the other side; then with the correct size drill bit all the way through. Drill a corresponding hole in the arm, 1in (25mm) from the front edge and 9½in (241mm) from the head. For extra flexibility, it is worth drilling a series of holes for the pin in the arm, around 2in (51mm) apart, and additional holes on the platform as well.

16 **Screw the platform to the bench**
Attach the platform to the bench with a pair of screws at the non-raised end, then further secure by drilling two more screws from underneath the bench up into the platform support.

MAKE A

WORKBENCH & POLE LATHE

This easy-to-construct workbench will provide a solid, stable surface for carrying out tasks such as sawing, drilling, and hammering. And if you decide to try your hand at wood turning, the bench provides a platform around which to construct a pole lathe.

YOU WILL NEED

TOOLS & EQUIPMENT

■ Pencil, long ruler, try square, sliding bevel, protractor, and spirit level

■ Handsaws (including a pull saw)

■ Electric drill with drill bits, including 1³⁄₁₆in (30mm) spade bit

■ Hacksaw

■ Metal file

■ Mortise chisel and small mallet

■ Drawknife and shaving horse

■ Mallet, froe, and wedges

■ Ax and ax block

■ Chalk line

■ F-clamps

■ Scrub plane

■ 1in (25mm) auger

■ 2 x wrenches or spanners

■ Straight knife

■ *optional*: Bench stop, metal crank, brace

MATERIALS

■ For the bench: 4 x 3m (9ft 10in) lengths of planed "2 x 4" planks

■ For the bench legs: 4 x billets split from a green wood log and shaped to about 40in (1016mm) long and 4in (102mm) wide, left to dry completely.

■ For the treadle: 1 green wood log, about 10⅝in (270mm) in diameter, and at least 44½in (1130mm) long

■ For the poppets: 1 green wood log, about 11in (279mm) in diameter and 26in (660mm) long

■ For the tool rest: 1 dry plank, 30½ x 2³⁄₁₆ x 1³⁄₁₆in (775 x 55 x 30mm)

■ For the wedges: 2 dry planks, 16 x ⅞ x 3¾in (406 x 23 x 95mm)

■ For the arms: 2 dry planks, 63 x 4 x 2in (1600 x 102 x 51mm), edges taken off

■ 2 dry wooden pegs, ⁹⁄₁₆in (14mm) in diameter and 6in (152mm) long

■ Bungee cord, about 160in (4.1m) long

■ Starter cord for motors, about 9ft (2.7m) long

■ M8 (⁵⁄₁₆in/ 8mm) threaded steel rod, enough for four sections just less than 14in (356mm) long, for the bench, and two sections 3½in (90mm) long, for the turning centers of the lathe

■ 8 x 1³⁄₁₆in (30mm) washers

■ 8 x ⁵⁄₁₆in (8mm) nuts, 4 x ⅜in (10mm) nuts

■ 5 x ⅜in (10mm) nuts and bolts for treadle

■ PVA glue

■ *optional*: Sheet of stiff plastic, for dovetail template

SKILLS

YOU WILL LEARN TO

■ Form countersink holes with a drill: *step 2*

■ Form a sliding dovetail joint: *steps 6–14*

■ Use a chalk line: *step 18*

REMIND YOURSELF HOW TO

■ Use an electric drill: *p24*

■ Use a pull saw: *p24*

■ Use a chisel: *p118*

■ Use a drawknife: *p94*

■ Level legs: *p154*

■ Split with a froe: *p82*

■ Shape with an ax: *p50*

■ Use a plane: *p100*

■ Use an auger: *p30*

KNIFE GRIP

■ Thumb pivot: *p22*

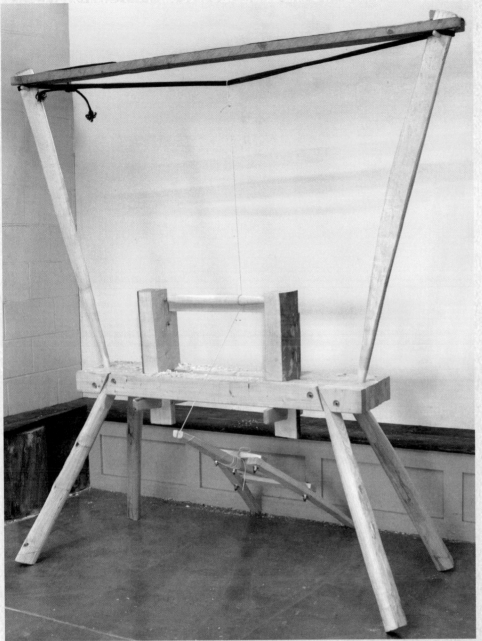

> **THE LEGS** FIT BY **SLIDING DOVETAIL JOINTS**, WHICH MAY LOOK TRICKY, BUT WITH THE **AID** OF **TEMPLATES** ARE IN FACT FAIRLY **SIMPLE TO ACHIEVE.**

DESIGN GUIDE

This design produces a substantial workbench by sandwiching together planks and slotting them onto metal bars. By inserting arms and poppets, and attaching string to bungee and treadle, the bench is quickly converted into a highly effective lathe.

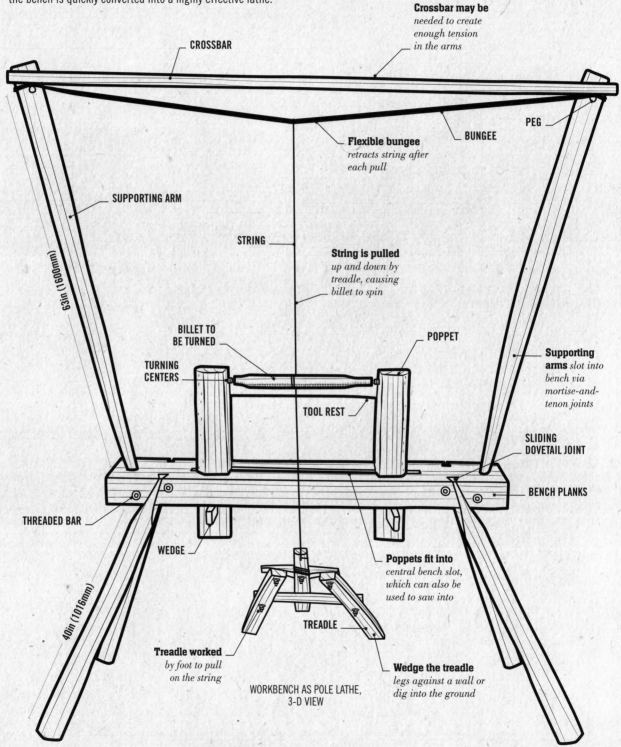

CROSSBAR

Crossbar may be *needed to create enough tension in the arms*

PEG

BUNGEE

Flexible bungee *retracts string after each pull*

SUPPORTING ARM

63in (1600mm)

STRING

String is pulled *up and down by treadle, causing billet to spin*

BILLET TO BE TURNED

POPPET

TURNING CENTERS

Supporting arms *slot into bench via mortise-and-tenon joints*

TOOL REST

SLIDING DOVETAIL JOINT

BENCH PLANKS

THREADED BAR

WEDGE

Poppets fit into *central bench slot, which can also be used to saw into*

40in (1016mm)

TREADLE

Treadle worked *by foot to pull on the string*

Wedge the treadle *legs against a wall or dig into the ground*

WORKBENCH AS POLE LATHE, 3-D VIEW

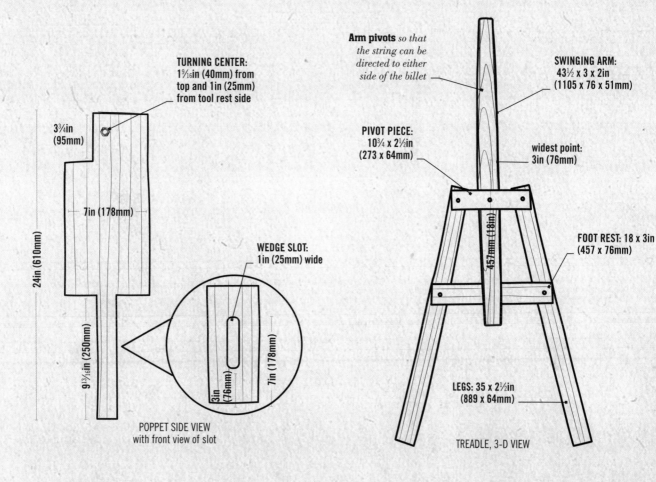

TURNING CENTER:
1⁹⁄₁₆in (40mm) from top and 1in (25mm) from tool rest side

3¾in (95mm)

7in (178mm)

24in (610mm)

9¹³⁄₁₆in (250mm)

WEDGE SLOT: 1in (25mm) wide

3in (76mm)

7in (178mm)

POPPET SIDE VIEW
with front view of slot

Arm pivots *so that the string can be directed to either side of the billet*

SWINGING ARM: 43½ x 3 x 2in (1105 x 76 x 51mm)

PIVOT PIECE: 10¾ x 2½in (273 x 64mm)

widest point: 3in (76mm)

457mm (18in)

FOOT REST: 18 x 3in (457 x 76mm)

LEGS: 35 x 2½in (889 x 64mm)

TREADLE, 3-D VIEW

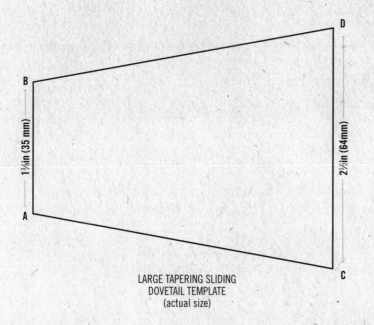

D

B

A

C

1³⁄₈in (35 mm)

2½in (64mm)

LARGE TAPERING SLIDING
DOVETAIL TEMPLATE
(actual size)

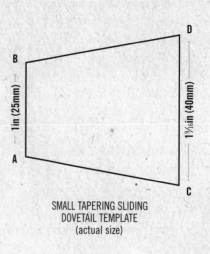

D

B

A

C

1in (25mm)

1⁹⁄₁₆in (40mm)

SMALL TAPERING SLIDING
DOVETAIL TEMPLATE
(actual size)

TIP

Hold the planks steady
on a suitable work surface;
straddling two ax blocks
allows you to saw into the
gap between.

The Process

Check the depth *of the countersink hole with a ruler*

1 Saw planks to length

Use a handsaw to cut three of the "2 x 4" planks in half, to give you six 4ft 9in (1.45m) lengths. Mark accurate lines with a ruler, pencil, and try square before sawing, and cut with a diagonal action. Saw two shorter pieces 12in (305mm) long from the remaining plank; these will form the midsection of the workbench, creating a slot for sawing into which also accommodates the pole lathe poppets.

2 Countersink holes for the nuts

Mark two crosses on one of the wide faces of a plank: the first at 4⁵⁄₁₆in (110mm) from the end and 1⅜in (35mm) in from the edge; the second 8⅞in (225mm) from the end and 1⅜in (35mm) in from the opposite edge. Cut holes at the crosses with the spade drill bit to a depth of ⅜in (10mm). Repeat at the other end to cut mirror image holes, then cut matching holes in a second plank.

Technique: Using an electric drill—see p24

Place a nut *on the bar for a guiding edge as you saw*

3 Drill through the planks

Mark the center of each countersink hole and drill straight through the plank at these points, using the ⅜in (10mm) bit. Measure and mark crosses at the corresponding points on all the other planks, including at one end of each of the two shorter ones, and drill holes straight through at these points as well. It is vital that all the holes match up and are drilled straight, since even a small misalignment will prevent the bar from threading all the way through the planks; using a drill bit with a slightly wider diameter than the rods provides some leeway.

4 Size the bar and file the ends

Cut the threaded bars slightly undersize, by ⅜in (10mm) less than combined thickness of the planks, since the final width of the bench will be narrower when the wood is compressed. Saw it off with a hacksaw in four equal lengths. Use a metal file to take the thread off the last ⅛in (3mm) at either end of each piece, and remove any sharp edges at the tips (*see left*).

CONTINUED ☞

File down
the ends of any bars that sit proud

5 Build up the bench

Attach a washer and nut on the end of each bar and insert them through the drilled holes of one of the countersunk planks. Turn the plank over so the bars point upward, spread wood glue down its length, and slot the next plank on top. Repeat for the remaining planks, attaching the shorter planks after the third long plank and remembering not to glue where the wood is exposed in the slot. Finish with the second countersunk plank and attach the washers and nuts.

6 Begin the leg mortises

First, mark a line along the upper surface of the bench, 7⅞in (200mm) from one end. Place the larger dovetail template on the upper surface, with point B on the 7⅞in (200mm) line and side AB along the edge of the bench, and draw round it. Turn the bench on its side and extend line B over the side, at an angle of 107° measured from the edge of the bench. On the underside of the bench, draw around the large template, aligning point A with the line just drawn.

TIP
Saw toward the center from both sides in turn—it's easier to get the joint looking neat this way.

Make sure
the lines don't intersect with the bolts

Aim to saw
precisely along the pencil lines

7 Mark the small template

Flip the bench back over and place the smaller template over the first, with point D of each aligned. Draw around it, then extend line AC to the edge of the bench, and continue the line over the side to meet point B of the large trapezium on the base. This shape will form a strong, sliding dovetail joint. Now mark all four mortises, remembering that opposing and adjacent pairs of joints should be mirror images of each other.

8 Saw down the sides

Use a pull saw to saw as accurately as you can down the sides of the mortise. Keep an eye on the alignment of the saw: you should be cutting along all three pencil lines on each face. Start sawing diagonally at a corner, then slowly angle the saw forward as you cut, so you end up sawing straight down. Stop exactly on the line at the base of the trapeziums. Saw down the other side.

Technique: Using a pull saw—see p24

CONTINUED ☞

Take care *not to chisel beyond the saw cuts*

Keep an eye out *for knots, which can damage your chisel*

Approach from above *and sides, but do not take material off the sides themselves*

9 Chop out the mortise

Starting at the thin end of the mortise, use a chisel and mallet to chop out small sections of wood. A sliding dovetail is designed to jam material in, so it is not always easy to chisel wood out. Line up the edge of the chisel with the pencil lines at the sides of the mortise. Tap down with the mallet until chips start to come out. Move down ⅜in (10mm) at a time with the chisel, then come around the other side of the mortise.

Technique: Using a chisel— see p118

10 Pare down

When you get close to the base of the mortise, switch to paring rather than chipping out. Hold the chisel with both hands, one low down and one near the top, supporting it against your chest. If using a square chisel, be very careful at the corners of the mortise, which are at tighter angles than the points of the chisel. Repeat steps 8–10 for the other mortises.

A stiff plastic *template gives a good edge to draw around*

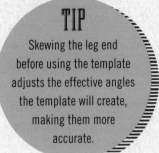

11 Begin leg tenon

Hold a leg against a mortise, so that the top of the leg is level with the top of the bench. Tilt the leg in turn to the angle of splay in both planes of the mortise, and draw corresponding lines on the leg to indicate the sloping section to be removed from the top. Saw this off, leaving an angled top. Place the large template on this sawed end and draw round it.

12 Shape the dovetail

On your shaving horse, use a drawknife to shape the leg tenon to the template. Start with the CD side of the trapezium, which will sit along the bottom face of the mortise, then cut AC and BD, before finishing with AB. Create parallel lines running down the leg from the four points of the trapezium, with flat faces between them. The tenon must be long enough to fit all the way into the mortise, so make your parallel lines extend about 2in (50mm) longer than the length of the mortise.

Technique: Using a draw knife—see p94

Check the width *down the leg with the large template*

CONTINUED ☞

> " BY TAPERING THE TENON TO
> ONE SIDE WE GAIN AS MUCH SPLAY
> AS POSSIBLE: AROUND 20°. "

Make sure that
*all the faces of
the leg are flat*

13 Taper the tenon
Place the small template on the end of the tenon, with point B of each trapezium aligned, and draw around it. You now need to shave an even taper down from the limit of the tenon to this new guideline; or in other words from the large trapezium down to the shape of the small trapezium at the tip of the tenon. The tenon must fit as tightly as possible at its limit, so do not make the taper longer than it needs to be. We are relying on the taper along the length of the tenon to create some of the splay, which makes cutting the mortise simpler as it can be straight backed.

14 Refine the tenon fit
Sharp corners can dig into the mortise and cause problems, so cut a thin chamfer off the edges of the tenon before fitting it. When testing the fit, make sure the back is aligned flat and adjust the sides as needed. All of the faces need to be flat; any roundness will create a pivot point, and there will not be enough surface contact between the mortise and tenon for a strong leg.

TIP
If one of the treadle billets has a curve to it, choose this for the swinging arm, which needs a slight curve anyway.

15 Assemble

Repeat for the other legs, checking they splay in the correct direction. Fit and level the legs, and saw off any protruding sections of tenon. Finally, drill holes along the center of the bench for bench stops and hold fasts. These are commonly ¾in (18.5mm) in diameter and set 2in (51mm) apart, but check the size of your hardware; you may prefer to drill as and when needed.

Technique: Leveling legs—see p154

Use a try square *to help drill straight*

16 Split out treadle billets

Take the treadle log and split out billets for the five pieces. Using a mallet, froe, and wedges, split the log in half, then into quarters down the radius, then split along the radius again to form wedges 2¾in (70mm) at their fattest point. Split these wedges in half again, but this time tangentially to leave triangular and quadrilateral wedges. Select the billets and saw them to length; avoid using the triangular billets from the center of the wood for longer pieces, as these tend to be more twisty and knotty.

Technique: Splitting with a froe—see p82

CONTINUED ☞

USING A CHALK LINE

1.

2.

A chalk line is a retractable length of string held i[n] a box filled with colored chalk, and is a great tool f[or] marking straight lines over uneven timber surface[s.]

1. Secure both ends of the chalk line and hold th[e] string taut over where you want to mark a guidelin[e]

2. Snap the string against the surface of the bil[let] to leave a colored chalk line. Here, the chalk line marks a center line to guide the shaping, but it ca[n] also be used to mark cutting edges.

Straighter sides make the pieces much easier to bolt

17 Shape the legs, footrest, and pivot

Take a quadrilateral wedge and form a leg piece for the treadle. Mark guide points indicating the width and chop out waste to these markers with an ax. Switch to the shaving horse and use a drawknife to take off the bark and shave to a more evenly rectangular cross section, with roughly straight edges and to the thickness indicated on p227, plus 15 percent to allow for shrinkage. Repeat with the other leg, footrest, and pivot cross-piece.

Technique: Shaping with an ax— see p50

18 Rough shape the arm

The swinging arm needs more careful shaping, so that it tapers at both ends and describes a gentle curve along its length. Make pencil marks indicating the width at either end, again allowing for shrinakge, then lay a chalk line down the center; *see above.* Mark on the widest point of the arm, which needs to sit halfway between the footrest and pivot, 18in (457mm) up from one end. Mark this with pencil guides and a chalk line. Follow these guides to ax the arm to size and, at the same time, shape a curved profile.

19 Hone the arm

Moving to the shaving horse, smooth off the ax cuts with a drawknife and accentuate the curve at the bottom end of the swinging arm. Cut a chamfer along all the edges of the rounded side and generally neaten. Don't go too thin at this stage, however, to allow for shrinkage. Leave all the treadle pieces to dry for about 2 weeks, then check the measurements and shave down further, if need be. Saw a notch centrally at what will be the top end of the swinging arm, 1in (25mm) deep and wide enough to hold the string securely.

Highlight in pencil *where you need to shave to curve the end*

20 Test the treadle fit

Drill ⅜in (10mm) holes for the bolts, at the points indicated on the design guide, using an electric drill. Do a dry run of bolting the pieces together and examine the treadle to see if there are any gaps between surfaces or if the swinging arm is being impeded in its movement. Make marks where any areas need shaving down (*see* right) and refine the fit on the shaving horse.

CONTINUED ☞

TIP
It can be helpful to alternate approaching from both ends with the froe when splitting off a thin section such as this.

When truing sides, *the ax is good for efficiency, but the drawknife is best for accuracy*

21 Split out the poppets

With a mallet and froe, split the log for the poppets in half. Follow the sizing guide on p227 to draw guidelines for splitting off the corners and a section of the pith and first few annular rings, to create two blocks of wood that will become the pole lathe's poppets.

22 Shave the sides square

Place the billets you are working on your bench, and use bench stops, or blocks of wood held with F-clamps, to hold them in place. Shave one of the two thinner sides flat, to set a datum surface. Using a ruler and try square, mark out and square the opposite side, followed by the bark-free face, from that datum. Hold a ruler against each side to check that they are flat.

23 Mark the tenon

On the face opposite the bark side, measure and mark a center line to the length of the poppet's tenon. Mark off the end of the tenon with a try square, then mark the thickness of the tenon with two more lines on either side of the center line; these are your saw lines. Extend them carefully around the sides and top of the billet, then saw down the lines at the end of the tenon with a handsaw.

Use a drawknife
to get the last little pieces at the back

24 Shape the tenon

Use the mallet and froe to remove the sides of the tenon; they should come away easily since you have already sawed off the ends. Instead of trying to remove the whole side in one shot, take off thin sections until just shy of the pencil line. Now clamp the billet on your bench, placing some spare pieces of wood beneath the tenon to support it. Use a scrub plane, and then a drawknife, to smooth down the sides of the tenon, removing the last $\frac{1}{16}$in (2mm) of wood so it is the right thickness to fit snugly into the bench.

Technique: Using planes—see p100

CONTINUED ☞

" IT IS VITAL THAT THE SIDES OF THE TOOL REST ARE PARALLEL ALONG ITS LENGTH. **"**

Flat sides
are important to give the wedge gripping surfaces

25 Make the tool rest
Take the 30½ x 2³⁄₁₆ x 1³⁄₁₆in (775 x 55 x 30mm) plank and clamp it on your shaving horse. Use a drawknife to carefully round off one edge by chamfering it at a 45° angle, and then smoothing out the chamfer to a curve by gradually taking off the corners. Do one half first then turn the plank around to shape the other half.

26 Make wedges for the poppets
Take one of the two 16 x ⅞ x 3¾in (406 x 23 x 95mm) planks. Draw a straight line on one of the flat faces, sloping from a corner to a point 2³⁄₁₆in (55mm) from the far side. Remove most of the narrower section with an ax, then use the drawknife to shave down to the line. Round off the sloped side with the drawknife and chamfer the ends. Repeat with the other plank.

TIP
The wedges should poke out a little on either side, but not so much that you might bang your knee on one.

27 Mark wedge slots on the poppets

Place the poppets at either end of the workbench slot. Hold up a wedge underneath the bench, against the inside face of the poppet, with a small amount extending beyond the side of the bench. Draw a pencil line on the poppet to mark the lower edge of the wedge. Remove the wedge and draw another pencil line on the poppet at the base of the bench. Remove the poppet and continue the lines around the face of the tenon; mark a center line on the face, too.

Hold the chisel *vertically and tap it down*

28 Drill and chisel the slot

Place some scrap wood underneath the tenon to hold it up, and clamp it to the bench. Using a 1in (25mm) auger, drill holes just shy of the two pencil marks you made; mark centerpoints for the auger by measuring ½in (12.5mm) in from each pencil line. For the lower hole, first drill straight down to bite into the wood, then bring the auger toward you to angle the hole inward. Drill more straight holes between the first two to form the slot, then chisel off the peaks left by the auger on the sides of the slot. Repeat on the other poppet.

CONTINUED ☞

TIP
It is worth wedging in the poppets before maing marks, to ensure they are in the correct position.

29 Mark holes for the centers

Place the poppets back in the bench slot and wedge in, to mark out holes for the turning centers of the lathe. Measure and mark the center point of the slot on one of the tenons, extending this point all the way up the center of the inner face of the poppet. The hole should be 1⁹⁄₁₆in (40mm) down from the top of the poppet: measure and mark a horizontal line at this point. Form the points of the centers by filing down one end of each metal bar to a sharp point, forming a cone about ⅛in (4mm) long (*see* right).

30 Drill center holes

Use a long ⅜in (10mm) drill bit to drill a hole through the poppet for the center. Make sure you are drilling parallel to the bench with a spirit level, and sight down the slot to drill parallel to the sides of the poppet. To drill the second poppet, clamp it right next to the first and use the drilled hole as a guide: drill through the first poppet again, then into the second, and straight through the other side. Place two ⅜in (10mm) nuts on the end of either center, tighten them against each other with two wrenches, then. screw them in tightly.

<blockquote>
❝ THE CENTERS NEED TO **LINE UP** PERFECTLY. ANY **WONKINESS** HERE WILL CAUSE THE LATHE TO **TURN UNEVENLY**. **❞**
</blockquote>

31 Mark lines for the tool rest platform

Wedge the poppets as far apart as they will go, while still being able to reach both with a ruler. Align the ruler with the center points and draw lines along the side of each poppet. Measure 2³⁄₁₆in (55mm)—or the height of your tool rest—down from that point, and draw more lines. Mark a vertical line 1in (25mm) out from the center on the inner face of each poppet, to give a wide platform for the tool rest.

32 Saw the platform

Use a handsaw to saw down the pencil lines, starting with the horizontal line where the base of the tool rest will sit. Then, with the poppets wedged into the bench slot, saw down the vertical line to the point where the two lines meet. Remove the excess chunks of wood.

Technique: Using a pull saw— see p24

CONTINUED ☞

TIP
Arm holes must be far
enough from the bench end
to avoid splitting the wood,
but not too close to the
metal bars.

33 Drill mortise holes for the arms

Draw a line 1¹⁵⁄₁₆in (50mm) from the end of the workbench and mark a cross at the midpoint for drilling the arm hole. Set a sliding bevel to an angle of 14° and drill a hole all the way through the bench at that angle, using a 1³⁄₁₆in (30mm) wood-cutting bit. Repeat to drill a hole for the second arm on the opposite end of the bench.

Ideally get someone to sight the angle

34 Shave cylindrical tenons on the arms

Back on the shaving horse, take shavings off the bottom end of each arm to form a smooth, cylindrical tenon. Start by making a square shape, then take off the corners to round it. For a snug fit, make sure the tenons are not flared out in any direction. Keep testing the fit and taking off more wood if needed, until you can get the first 1in (25mm) or so into the mortise hole; then shave the full length of the tenon to match. The tenons should go all the way through the bench and sit a little proud underneath it. Finish them by putting a heavy chamfer on the ends, with a straight knife held in thumb pivot grip.

35 Drill holes in the arms

Using a ⁹⁄₁₆in (14mm) auger or drill bit in your electric drill, or a brace if you have one, drill a hole at the center of the top end of each arm. Make sure you drill far enough from the end to avoid splitting, but do not go too low, or there won't be enough space for you to stand under the string of the pole lathe; 3½in (90mm) from the end should be sufficient. Drill about 95 percent of the way through—the lead screw should just poke out on the other side—then turn the plank over and finish drilling from the other side. This avoids tearout, giving you a neat hole.

36 Fashion pegs and an optional crossbar

Make non-tapering wooden pegs ⁹⁄₁₆in (14mm) long and tap them into the arm holes with a mallet; these are to hold up the bungee as the string pulls on it. Finally, make an optional crossbar to help strengthen the arms by sawing a roughly central V-notch into either end of the plank. You may first need to adjust the length of the plank, depending on the fit of the arms.

CONTRIBUTORS

ROBIN DUCKMANTON (CAPTAIN'S CHAIR)

Robin is a professional chairmaker based in North Yorkshire, UK. He has been a maker for 10 years, concentrating solely on chairs for the last five. He first learned frame chairmaking from Mike Abbott, then went to Tennessee to learn the art of American Colonial Windsor chairmaking from Curtis Buchanan. He makes and teaches from a wooden cabin at the end of his garden, using wood sourced from some of the highest-quality furniture-making woodland in the UK.
redwoodchairs.co.uk
Instagram: @redwoodchairs

TOM HEPWORTH (BOWL)

Graduating from the prestigious Falmouth School of Art, UK, Tom specialized in video editing before apprenticing with Barn the Spoon. He then helped establish The Green Wood Guild in London and now divides his time between making and teaching woodcraft. His work is focused on producing beautiful household items as "functional sculpture," grounded in traditional heritage crafts.

SOPHIE RIDLEY (FRAME STOOL)

Born and raised in Leeds, Sophie went on to complete a BA in Fine Art at Central Saint Martins. While studying, she explored interests in environmental art, collective practice, and more traditional craft. Since graduating, Sophie has remained in London, working in museums and galleries while also training in furniture design and art therapy with Barn the Spoon.

HARRY SAMUEL (TURNING)

After training at The Green Wood Guild and completing an apprenticeship at The Cherry Wood Project, Harry is now a full-time green wood craftsman and woodland worker based in the south west of the UK. He manages woodland to supply the raw materials for his work crafting treen, green wood furniture, and timber frames.
Instagram: @sparry_hoons

TIM SANDERSON (JOINERY)

Tim earned a first class degree in Graphic Design at Kingston University London, where his fascination with materials and how things work led him to woodwork. Tim now teaches joinery and furniture making at The Green Wood Guild, and has a passion for turning bowls.

MORE ABOUT SPOONS

Spoonclub
Barn the Spoon set up his first Spoonclub with friends in 2010 as a place where people could get together to carve. There is now a growing number of clubs worldwide with a website where you can find your local club, buy tools and blanks, and subscribe to a large number of professionally produced video tutorials, which demonstrate everything from the real basics to advanced carving.
spoonclub.co.uk

SPOON: A GUIDE TO SPOON CARVING AND THE NEW WOOD CULTURE (SCRIBNER, 2017)
Read more about spoon carving in this, Barn's first book, where he lays out his manifesto for making, and gives the reader a firm foundation in not just the techniques, but also the thinking behind the functional beauty of 16 different traditional styles of wooden spoons.

ACKNOWLEDGMENTS

From the author
For the pulled fiber brush and cutting board inspiration:

JARROD DAHL FROM THE UNITED STATES
Instagram: @woodspirithandcraft

For the coffee bag clip inspiration:

LEE SEIL FROM THE REPUBLIC OF KOREA
Instagram: @iseilnam

From the publisher
We would like to acknowledge the help of the following people in the production of this book: thanks to Louise Brigenshaw, Karen Constanti, Mandy Earey, and Simon Murrell for design assistance; Steve Crozier for repro work; Kathy Steer for editorial assistance; Marie Lorimer for indexing; and David Fisher, US consultant, for his work in ensuring that the technical details are correct for North American readers. Thanks also to Katie Abbott for kindly hosting us at her patch of woodland in Essex and providing such an inspirational day of green woodworking at the very start of the project.

Picture credits
The publisher would like to thank the following for their kind permission to reproduce their photograph:
9 Alamy Stock Photo: Miriam Heppell
All other images © Dorling Kindersley
For further information see: www.dkimages.com

> **66** BARNABY CARDER SPEAKS ABOUT SPOONS **MORE PASSIONATELY** THAN MOST PEOPLE SPEAK ABOUT ANYTHING. **99** – THE DAILY TELEGRAPH

ABOUT THE AUTHOR

BARN THE SPOON

Barnaby Carder opened his infamous London-based spoon shop in 2012 and his work popularizing spoon carving has earned him much international acclaim. Barn's collaborations, such as Spoonfest and Spoonclub, have helped raise the reputation of the humble wooden spoon. In *Woodcraft*, Barn builds on 20 years of craft and teaching, and his collaborations at The Green Wood Guild, to create a project list with the aim of inspiring readers to get involved with woodcraft and show them how.

Barn runs regular spoon-carving workshops in London; to book a class or buy spoons visit: **barnthespoon.com**

THE GREEN WOOD GUILD

A little woodworking school founded in central London, The Green Wood Guild teaches woodcraft to Londoners and the many international students it attracts. The Guild not only provides skilled teaching, but also respite for the city dwellers. People can come as a one-off to try out a short whittling workshop, but most then decide to complete the set of classes available, which include: bowl carving, furniture making, and knife forging. **thegreenwoodguild.com**

DISCLAIMER

Neither the author nor the publisher take any responsibility for any injury or damage resulting from the use of techniques shown or described in this book. The reader is advised to follow all safety instructions carefully, wear the correct protective clothing, and, where appropriate, follow all manufacturers' instructions.